THE OLD HOUSE

TIME
LIFE ®
BOOKS

Other Publications:
YOUR HOME
THE ENCHANTED WORLD
THE KODAK LIBRARY OF CREATIVE PHOTOGRAPHY
GREAT MEALS IN MINUTES
THE CIVIL WAR
PLANET EARTH
COLLECTOR'S LIBRARY OF THE CIVIL WAR
THE EPIC OF FLIGHT
THE GOOD COOK
THE SEAFARERS
WORLD WAR II
THE OLD WEST

For information on and a full description of any of the Time-Life
Books series listed above, please write:

Reader Information
Time-Life Books
541 North Fairbanks Court
Chicago, Illinois 60611

This volume is part of a series offering homeowners
detailed instructions on repairs, construction
and improvements they can undertake themselves.

HOME REPAIR
AND IMPROVEMENT

THE OLD HOUSE

BY THE EDITORS OF
TIME-LIFE BOOKS

TIME-LIFE BOOKS
ALEXANDRIA, VIRGINIA

Time-Life Books Inc.
is a wholly owned subsidiary of
TIME INCORPORATED

Founder	Henry R. Luce 1898-1967
Editor-in-Chief	Henry Anatole Grunwald
President	J. Richard Munro
Chairman of the Board	Ralph P. Davidson
Corporate Editor	Jason McManus
Group Vice President, Books	Reginald K. Brack Jr.
Vice President, Books	George Artandi

TIME-LIFE BOOKS INC.

Editor	George Constable
Executive Editor	George Daniels
Editorial General Manager	Neal Goff
Director of Design	Louis Klein
Editorial Board	Dale M. Brown, Roberta Conlan, Ellen Phillips, Gerry Schremp, Gerald Simons, Rosalind Stubenberg, Kit van Tulleken, Henry Woodhead
Director of Photography	John Conrad Weiser
President	William J. Henry
Senior Vice President	Christopher T. Linen
Vice Presidents	Stephen L. Bair, Robert A. Ellis, John M. Fahey Jr., Juanita T. James, James L. Mercer, Joanne A. Pello, Paul R. Stewart, Christian Strasser

HOME REPAIR AND IMPROVEMENT

Editorial Staff for The Old House

Editor	Robert M. Jones
Assistant Editor	Mark M. Steele
Designer	Kenneth E. Hancock
Chief Researchers	Oobie Gleysteen, Phyllis Wise
Picture Editor	Neil Kagan
Text Editors	Leslie Marshall, Lydia Preston, Brooke Stoddard, David Thiemann
Staff Writers	Lynn R. Addison, William C. Banks, Megan Barnett, Robert A. Doyle, Malachy Duffy, Steven J. Forbis, Peter Pocock, William Worsley
Copy Coordinators	Margery duMond, Brian Miller
Art Associates	George Bell, Lorraine D. Rivard, Richard Whiting
Picture Coordinator	Renée DeSandies
Editorial Assistant	Susan Larson

Editorial Operations

Design	Ellen Robling (assistant director)
Copy Room	Diane Ullius
Editorial Operations	Caroline A. Boubin (manager)
Production	Celia Beattie
Quality Control	James J. Cox (director), Sally Collins
Library	Louise D. Forstall

Correspondents: Elisabeth Kraemer-Singh (Bonn); Margot Hapgood, Dorothy Bacon (London); Miriam Hsia, Susan Jonas, Lucy T. Voulgaris (New York); Maria Vincenza Aloisi, Josephine du Brusle (Paris); Ann Natanson (Rome). Valuable help was also given by: Enid Farmer (Boston); Judy Aspinall, Lesley Coleman, Karin B. Pearce (London); Carolyn T. Chubet, Christina Lieberman (New York); Mimi Murphy (Rome).

Time-Life Books Inc. offers a wide range of fine recordings, including a *Rock 'n' Roll Era* series. For subscription information, call 1-800-621-7026 or write Time-Life Music, P.O. Box C-32068, Richmond, Virginia 23261-2068.

THE CONSULTANTS: Charles Miller, who works as a house inspector in White Plains, New York, has supervised heavy construction projects for more than 40 years. He is a former member of the Architectural Board of Review of Mamaroneck, New York.

Claxton Walker, who was a home builder and remodeler for more than two decades in Maryland, Virginia and the District of Columbia, now inspects homes for prospective buyers. A former industrial arts teacher, he lectures before real estate brokers and the public on spotting problems in older homes. He has written magazine and newspaper articles and co-authored books on home inspection and residential energy conservation.

Roswell W. Ard, a civil engineer, is a consulting structural engineer and a home inspector who has written professional papers on wood-frame construction techniques. He has designed heating, electrical and motor-control systems, and has explored alternate energy systems, including solar-energy and wind-power generators.

Harris Mitchell, special consultant for Canada, has worked in the field of home repair and improvement for more than two decades. He is Homes editor of *Today* magazine and author of a syndicated newspaper column, "You Wanted to Know," as well as a number of books on home improvement.

Library of Congress Cataloguing in Publication Data
Time-Life Books.
    The old house
    (Home repair and improvement)
    Includes index.
    1. Dwellings — Remodeling.   I.Title.
TH4816.T55   1979a   643'.7   79-18936
ISBN 0-8094-2424-X
ISBN 0-8094-2423-1 lib. bdg.
ISBN 0-8094-2422-3 retail ed.

Contents

LIGHTS ON
O & K
O & X
O only
K only
K & X
None

INDICATION
Correct Wiring
Reversed Polarity
Reversed Ground
Open Ground
Open Neutral
Reversed Hot & Gnd
Open Hot

From Relic to Residence

At first sight, a stately old house often evokes romantic feelings and a sense of nostalgia, but everyday living in a house built by men who voted for President Taft—or Washington—can quickly arouse more practical concerns for safety, convenience and economy.

Living in an old house is a compromise between preservation and practicality. However tempting fast cosmetic repairs might be, more serious flaws such as deteriorated structural timbers or masonry may have to be given top priority. A thorough inspection of an old house will allow you to estimate the gravity of major problems before you buy, and will help you establish practical work priorities afterward. A leaking roof, for example, should be remedied as soon as possible, not only for comfort but to prevent further water damage inside the house. For safety, frayed electrical wiring should be put into top condition—or replaced—immediately. Since fixing faulty plumbing often requires that you open walls and ceilings, worn-out pipes should be replaced in the earliest stages of a renovation. In most areas of the country, heating also must have high priority. Make sure your furnace is operating well long before cold weather arrives; if you do not yet own the house, verify during your inspection—which is the subject of this chapter—that the furnace is in good condition.

In addition to inspecting the house itself, evaluate the neighborhood. Find out if other nearby homes are already being fixed up or entirely renovated—usually an indication that property values will rise. Visit the neighborhood at different times of the day: at rush hour you may find excessive traffic in front of the house; a swing by on a Sunday evening, when most people are at home, should give you an idea of parking availability. You will, of course, also check such obvious plus values as good police and fire protection, low taxes, convenient schools and commuting, and the like.

Whether you want to fix up most of the house yourself or intend to hire professionals for much of the work, plan carefully. Commit your plans to paper long before work begins, taking into account the extent of the work needed at each phase of the job, what you can realistically afford and when each task should be completed. When you set up a timetable for work you plan to do yourself, allow for unforeseen delays—an object or material that must be specially ordered, for example, or just bad weather on a day you planned to work outdoors. Have a list of alternative indoor projects if outdoor work is rained out. To avoid delays, assemble all materials and tools needed before beginning a project. If you plan to work an entire day, do the heavy jobs in the morning, when you are strongest and most alert, and reserve less demanding tasks for the afternoon, when mistakes due to fatigue are most common.

The Evolution of American House Construction

In evaluating an old house—both for existing problems and for possible improvements—you need an understanding of its basic structure. Because the framework is hidden behind finished surfaces, it may seem mysterious and complex; in fact, however, the basic methods of house construction are quite straightforward and have undergone very few fundamental changes since colonial times.

The first frame houses—as distinct from log houses—appeared in the northern colonies in the 1630s. Employing a design and techniques developed in the Middle Ages, colonial carpenters notched and pegged together massive posts and beams to assemble a formidable boxlike frame atop a fieldstone or brick foundation. Although most timbers in the colonial frame house were much heavier than their modern counterparts, the floor joists were smaller; therefore a huge "summer" beam (from the French *somme*, meaning "burden"), almost a foot square in cross section, was centered in any span exceeding 20 feet.

To this standard medieval framework, colonial builders added their invention of exterior sheathing—typically of wide boards 1 inch thick nailed horizontally to the studs. Lapped clapboards or shingles, particularly resistant to harsh American winters, often covered this sheathing to complete the construction of a typical colonial braced-frame house, so called for its diagonal corner braces.

Although the braced-frame house was most common, by the mid 1600s brick houses were also being built, particularly in Virginia and New Amsterdam (later New York), where the clay soil proved suitable for brickmaking. Though colonial masonry construction dates back to the 1600s, it was expensive and did not become widespread until the second half of the 19th Century, when bricks and blocks could be mass-produced efficiently. However, the basic design, which combines bearing walls of brick or stone with interior wood framing set into pockets in the masonry, has remained essentially unchanged for some 300 years.

The heavy post-and-beam configuration of the braced-frame house remained basically unchallenged until a Yankee architect named Augustine Deodat Taylor revolutionized housebuilding by inventing the balloon frame, in Chicago in 1833. The balloon frame—so named by skeptics who compared the stud walls with the skin of a balloon—employed only small timbers (such as 2-by-4 studs) but placed them close together so they could bear the same weight as the heavier, more widely spaced posts and beams.

Two 19th Century technological developments made the balloon frame possible: the invention of the circular mill saw and the mass production of nails. The circular saw permitted accurate cutting of small timbers, and nailed joints replaced hand-cut joints to allow swift construction by unskilled laborers. Widely adopted in booming 19th Century Chicago, the balloon frame raced westward and became the standard building method in thousands of prairie towns.

Shortly after the turn of the 20th Century a final modification of the balloon frame emerged—the western, or platform, frame. The long 2-by-4 studs that rose from the foundation sill plate all the way to the second- or third-floor rafters were replaced by shortened studs topped by an intermediate plate at each story. The shorter studs—virtually identical to those used today—were easier to handle and workmen could use the completed first-story frame as a platform for constructing the second-story framing.

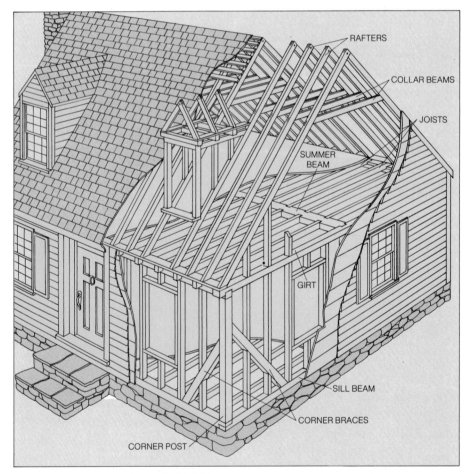

The colonial braced-frame house. In this 18th Century house, four massive sill beams, lap-jointed at the corners, rest on a stone foundation wall. Strong vertical posts at the corners and along front and rear walls support four horizontal beams, called girts, which serve as second-story plates. A huge summer beam—running the length of the house and notched into the girts at each end—gives extra support for second-floor joists; diagonal braces reinforce each corner. The rafters meet at the peak in pegged mortise-and-tenon joints and are braced by collar beams.

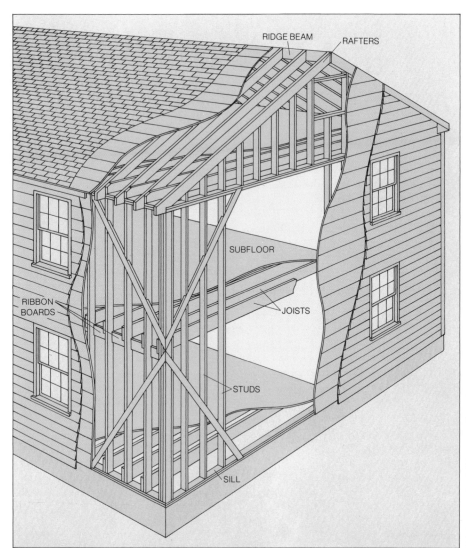

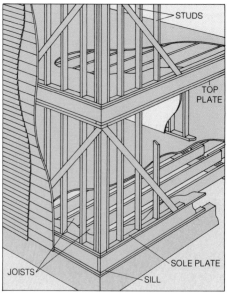

The balloon frame. This balloon-frame house relies for its support on small timbers nailed in place. The 2-by-4 wall studs, on 16-inch centers, rise unbroken from the sills to the rafters; at the corners, 2-by-4s are nailed together to form posts. The 2-by-8 floor joists nailed to the studs are supported by sills at the first-floor level and by ribbon boards—1-by-4s notched into the studs—at higher floors. The rafters are nailed to a ridge beam at the peak.

In western, or platform, framing *(detail, below)* the joists and subfloor are laid first, then 2-by-4 studs the height of only one story go between a single 2-by-4 sole plate and a doubled 2-by-4 top plate. The joists, subfloor and stud walls of the second floor are stacked onto the framing of the first floor in the same way.

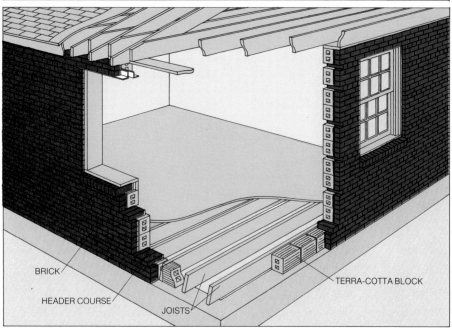

A solid-masonry house. The walls of this early 20th Century masonry bungalow consist of a single thickness, or wythe, of hollow terra-cotta block covered by a layer of brick. (In older houses, some dating from the colonial period, the inner layer is usually brick instead of terra-cotta block.) The brick is mortared to the blocks and at regular intervals—in this case every seventh course —a header course of bricks is laid down perpendicular to the wall between block courses to further secure the bricks to the blocks. Floor joists are set on top of the foundation wall between blocks. In many houses, first-floor joists are supported in the center of their span by a girder over a masonry pier.

In many modern wood-frame houses, a layer of nonstructural brick veneer is secured to the sheathing and studs with metal ties to give the house a masonry exterior.

Inspecting an Old House before You Buy

Evaluating an old house is always a process of compromise. The need for minor repairs like painting, refinishing floors and freeing stuck windows may disqualify a house if its over-all appeal to you is only marginal, while major work like foundation and roofing repairs may seem acceptable if you have found a truly exceptional old house.

Fortunately for impulsive buyers, many old houses are remarkably sound; in bygone eras the cost of top-grade materials and labor was low and pride in craftsmanship was high. But making a thorough and objective inspection of any house that you are seriously considering buying is a wise approach for two reasons: to make sure there are no fatal flaws that preclude buying at all, and to arrive at a realistic estimate of the renovations you will have to face.

If you are really interested in a house, be firm in your request for at least two hours to make a detailed inspection, even if the seller seems cool to the idea. The seller will want to display the best features of the house; your responsibility as buyer is to discover the worst. The inspection is primarily visual, but assemble these few simple tools as aids: binoculars for examining details on the roof, an ice pick or awl to probe rotting wood, a flashlight, a tape measure or folding rule, a plug-in analyzer for checking electrical outlets, a small magnet to test types of metal in plumbing and other fixtures, a 15-foot length of string and some thumbtacks for checking any sag or bulge in framing, matches for checking the draft in a furnace flue, and a pencil and paper to keep notes.

As you approach the house, notice its general surroundings and its orientation to the sun. A house that is much grander or much more modest than others in the neighborhood may not be a good financial risk. As for the sun, year-round energy savings are greatest when large windows have a southern exposure, and strategically placed trees serve as buffers against both the heat of a summer afternoon and prevailing winds. On the other hand, a house that is nestled in thick woods may always be slightly damp and prone to moisture damage and rot. Also consider the over-all security of the house, noting the visibility and accessibility of the doors and windows and the type of fences.

Your evaluation of the exterior of the house should pivot primarily on how well it repels water, and the first area to scrutinize is the roof. Examine the condition of the roof surface itself, and note its slope—a roof that has a steep pitch is less likely to leak but is more difficult to repair than one with a gentle pitch. Focus your binoculars on roof areas that are particularly vulnerable to leaks, such as joints between converging slopes and around chimneys, and any exposed flashing. Even when a roof does not leak, water channeled off it improperly can cause damage, so inspect all gutters and downspouts, especially any sections under tree branches where the acidity of wet fallen leaves may have eaten through. Gutter runs that are longer than 40 feet should have two downspouts.

Check next for damage to exterior walls. In masonry walls look for areas with lighter mortar—a sign of patching—and for crumbling mortar that will require repair. A section of rotted wood siding can be patched with fiberglass and repainted, provided there is enough good wood left to secure the patch to the wall.

Question local exterminators about the most common insects in the area and check along the walls and foundation for infestations. Termites, carpenter ants and powder-post beetles can cause serious structural damage, while the presence of other insects such as fleas and ticks—both notoriously difficult to cope with—may result in the additional expense of hiring a professional exterminator.

Throughout every phase of the inspection, evaluate your findings in two ways: Note the extent of any immediately visible damage, then trace the long-term, less obvious effects of the damage on other parts of the house. Badly damaged chimney flashing, for example, is unsightly and may be a source of leaks, but it may indicate even more serious trouble: past leaking may have damaged the framing, insulation, wiring and interior finish of the house. In the same way, correlate symptoms to pinpoint seemingly mysterious problems. The most obvious source of water damage on a plaster ceiling is a leaky roof, but missing tiles and caulking in a bathroom overhead could also be the source of the problem.

Use the same techniques to evaluate any secondary structures on the property as well as the house itself. Inspect porches for leaks in their shallow-pitched roofs, or for rot and termites where their wood framing touches the ground. Make certain garage doors work well, and that there is a 4-inch step down to an attached garage to prevent gasoline fumes—which are heavier than air—from leaking into the house.

Next examine the ground level at the foundation to see that it has been graded so it noticeably slopes away from the house for at least 6 feet. If it is level or slopes down toward the foundation, look for signs of a wet basement and foundation damage. You can correct improper grading by filling in earth around the foundation, but this may mean uprooting and replanting shrubbery.

Check for dead or dying trees that will require the services of professional tree surgeons. If limbs have been pruned back at least 6 feet from the house, potential damage from falling branches is reduced, as is the likelihood of gutters clogging with leaves. Examine all walkways and driveways for cracks and sinking; generally, displacements greater than 1 inch are hazardous and beyond repair, and call for repaving. Any low points in a driveway should have a functioning drain, particularly if the driveway slopes toward the house. Check that any retaining walls do not bulge or lean noticeably, and that they have drainage holes—known as weep holes—that allow water to flow through. A wall that leans more than 1 inch laterally for every vertical foot may have to rebuilt.

Starting at the Top

Critical areas on the roof. Using binoculars, inspect the entire roof, looking particularly at the south side—the side most exposed to the sun—and analyze the condition of the roof surface itself according to type (below). Check for any sag along the ridge. Look at the gable end to see if there are already two or more layers of shingles; if so, you will have to remove the old roofing before reroofing. Inspect all exposed flashing around the chimney, in roof valleys and around any protruding pipes. Bent, rusted or cracked flashing or separations along gutters require immediate attention and should alert you to look for corresponding water damage inside.

On a freestanding exterior chimney, inspect the joint between the side of the house and the chimney. If the chimney has pulled away from the house to create a separation that widens to as much as 3 inches at the top, the chimney footing is failing and you should consult a foundation engineer. Smaller cracks are probably due to gradual settling, but they should be watched for any enlargement.

Mortar failure in a chimney, a common source of leaks, is a fire hazard as well, since sparks may escape into wood framing. In both exterior and interior chimneys, look for loose or damaged bricks, gaps in mortar joints, or a cracked and chipped chimney cap. These defects should be remedied before the chimney is used.

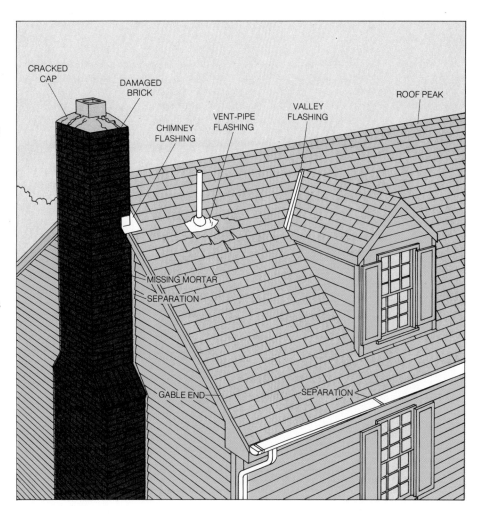

CRACKED CAP

DAMAGED BRICK

CHIMNEY FLASHING

VENT-PIPE FLASHING

VALLEY FLASHING

ROOF PEAK

MISSING MORTAR

SEPARATION

GABLE END

SEPARATION

Estimating the Life of a Roof

A double sample of each of four types of roofs shows typical signs of deterioration (left) and sound roofing (right).

Asphalt. Look for loss of the gravel coating, and for curled and torn shingles. Typically, asphalt shingles last 20 years, but if more than 25 per cent are damaged you may need to reroof soon.

Slate. This sound slate could last 40 years; more expensive slate may last 100 years. Flaking and white stains indicate about 10 more useful years.

Wood shingles. Cedar shingles often last 35 years. Deteriorated shingles must be replaced at once, while those in good condition could last another 20 years.

Metal. A metal roof may last 50 years. The old roof, though patched, is still pitted and worn. The new roof has a good seal at a vent and shows no deterioration.

Asphalt

Slate

Wood shingles

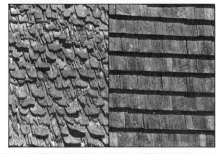

Metal

Faulty gutters and downspouts. Place a magnet against a downspout to find out what the metal is; the magnet will hold to galvanized steel—the most common type of gutter on old houses—but not to copper, which is less common but longer lasting. Examine galvanized gutters for rust spots and breaks in the metal, and copper gutters for holes or pitting. Check either type for separation along the back seam of the downspout—generally caused by clogging and freezing. Step away from the house and examine the position of each gutter in relation to the fascia board behind it—gutters should slope slightly toward the downspouts. Check that the splash blocks below downspouts are in good condition and are positioned to direct water away from the foundation; make sure that any drainpipes below the downspouts are not clogged.

Wherever you spot a fault in a gutter system, examine the nearby soffit and fascia board, the siding below, and the wood framing at ground level. Look for peeling paint, dark rot spots or other signs of water damage.

Evaluating the Walls

Scrutinizing wood siding. From each corner of the house, sight down the horizontal lines of the siding for any dip in the boards at the far corner; a noticeable dip indicates a sinking corner, often caused by rot or insect damage in the wood framing inside the wall or by a sinking foundation. This constitutes a serious structural problem and requires consultation with a structural engineer and, possibly, expensive repairs.

Examine the siding boards for curling and cracking and probe any rotted-looking areas; if your metal probe penetrates easily more than ½ inch, the rot needs repair. You can nail slightly bowed boards back in place and patch small areas of rot with fiberglass (pages 96-97), but extensive rot or cracks all the way through the board along more than half its length call for replacement with new boards. Check the existing paint: The more layers there are, the harder it will be to achieve a smooth finish with new paint.

Spotting a faulty brick wall. Sight along the exterior of the wall for bulging in the brick, especially near the bottom of the wall and midway up the wall near windows. Bulges indicate mortar failure in solid-masonry construction or deteriorated ties between brick veneer and the frame of a house. Although they generally affect only the area where they occur and rarely threaten the entire house, these bulges may still require major work in a few years.

Probe mortar joints with an ice pick. If the mortar seems soft and sandy and falls out easily, you must undertake the time-consuming job of scraping and refilling the joints to maintain the wall.

Evaluating bulges in stucco walls. Examine stucco walls at an oblique angle in order to spot bulges. Press lightly to test the springiness of small bulges—generally caused by localized separation between the stucco and underlying lath—and listen for a hollow sound when you tap them. If an entire wall bulges out at the center, the house may have a major structural flaw—either uneven settlement of the foundation or undersized framing members that will require strengthening. All bulges and major cracks in stucco should be repaired as soon as possible, to prevent water damage inside the wall.

Detecting insect damage. Along foundation walls and wherever wood members are near the ground—as in a crawl space with a dirt floor —look for termite tubes, signs of boring, or small piles of fine sawdust. Also note evidence of previous termite treatment: ¾-inch-diameter holes refilled with mortar in masonry walls or in the concrete floor of a basement. Prior treatment is not necessarily a bad sign, for it may have been done to forestall termites, and it may include a long-term guarantee.

Probe the wood framing in any areas where you suspect present or past infestation. The presence of termite shields—metal barriers installed between the foundation and framing (inset) —should not deter you from your inspection, since such shields are often ineffective.

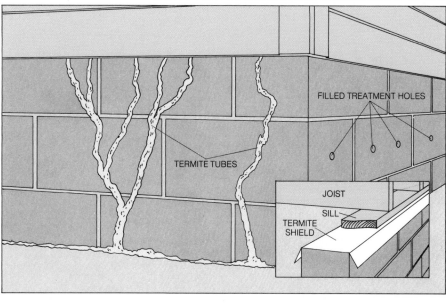

Is the Basement Snug and Dry?

A basement inspection provides an excellent opportunity to check the basic structural soundness of a house, since both the foundation and the framing members are often visible. For the best evaluation, correlate the flaws you see in these two areas; small foundation cracks in an old house, for instance, are probably insignificant if the framing members—joists, sill plates and girders—appear straight and solid. This type of crack typically occurs during early foundation settling or develops gradually over many years.

Large cracks that have no old paint or dust inside them—or are filled with different shades of mortar, a sign of recurrent patching—indicate newer and more serious structural damage and are usually accompanied by visible sagging or tilting in the framing. To evaluate these cracks it is best to consult a foundation engineer.

If the drainage around a house is poor, even small foundation cracks will allow ground water to seep in. If a basement is obviously wet or shows evidence of flooding, you may have to correct outside grading or gutter faults, patch the inside of a foundation wall, seal the wall on the outside or, in extreme cases, install a sump pump.

Detecting signs of flooding. While examining basement floors and walls for water stains, use a flashlight to check for rust stains and mud under the furnace—a telltale clue frequently overlooked by owners who have repainted to disguise evidence of flooding. Throughout the basement look on the walls for efflorescence (rough white deposits caused by water reacting with the minerals in mortar); look at any low-lying woodwork, such as baseboards, for dark spots of rot; and check tile floors for white powdery deposits—efflorescence from the underlying concrete. Note how things are stored: Unused furniture and storage boxes kept on shelves or raised platforms usually imply frequent flooding.

Analyzing cracks. Horizontal cracks in the middle of a basement wall accompanied by noticeable bulging inward indicate excessive pressure exerted by the ground outside the wall, caused by water pressure in the soil or compaction due to nearby recent construction, such as a new brick wall in the yard. Vertical cracks in a corner of the basement that widen to ¼ inch or more at the top are typically caused by a sinking footing beneath the foundation. Since either type of cracking can threaten the integrity of an entire wall, you should consult a foundation engineer for a precise diagnosis. Smaller cracks—common in old houses—pose no threat to the structure but may be a source of leaks.

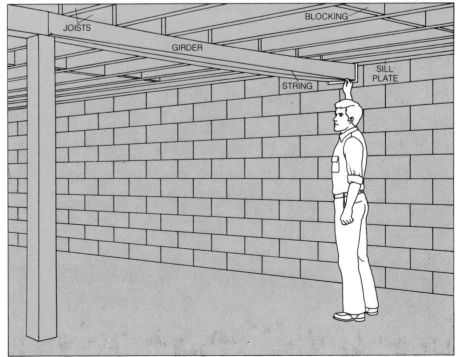

Examining wood framing. Measure any noticeable sag in a girder or joist by tacking a string taut between opposite bottom corners of the member; a sag greater than 1 inch in 12 feet calls for additional support beneath that joist or girder. Examine all exposed framing members—joists, girders, sill plates, and the subfloor above (if any)—for rot or insect damage. Also check for solid blocking or X-shaped bracing between joists, which indicates sturdy construction.

Is the Attic Weathertight?

Looking at the attic is often a highly informative part of a house inspection because the underside of the roof and its frame, as well as wiring, ducts and insulation, are exposed to view. When checking for roof leaks in the attic, remember that water flows unpredictably down framing members; look for dark, discolored wood and rust streaks around nailheads to trace this flow. Correlate any water paths you detect in the attic with your findings during your inspection of the finished interior *(pages 16-17)*.

Proper ventilation and insulation are both essential in an attic. Otherwise, condensation that forms in winter when the warm house air meets the cool attic air may cause moisture damage to framing, insulation and wiring; and in summer, hot air from an unvented attic will radiate down into the house. Check that existing vents—along the ridge or at the gable ends—are unobstructed. If there are no vents, look for moisture damage.

Throughout the attic inspection, note the available storage space and the feasibility of a later conversion to living space. In a row house, where masonry walls between houses are shared, the masonry should rise to the roof to serve as a fire wall separating your attic from those adjacent to it.

Evaluating attic insulation. In an unfinished attic, insert a ruler between the exposed joists to measure the thickness of any insulation. For energy efficiency, temperate climates require at least a 6-inch thickness of insulation. If there is new blanket or batt insulation, make sure the shiny foil or plastic vapor barrier faces down, toward the warmth of the house.

To check the insulation in a finished attic, look for knot holes on missing floorboards near the bottoms of rafters or in the backs of closets.

Poor insulation in the attic may mean inadequate insulation in the walls below. It is often hard to check wall insulation because the insulating material will have settled and compacted. However, by removing an electrical outlet cover, you can sometimes glimpse inside a wall to find out what insulation, if any, it contains.

Inspecting the roof framing. Examine all structural members for signs of rot, insects or water damage, probing suspect areas with an ice pick. If more than four consecutive rafters are rotted, rebuilding of the roof may be in order; consult a professional. Look for rust streaks from nailheads, and for other water stains, on the roof sheathing and around chimneys or vent stacks. Make sure that vent pipes—for plumbing or a kitchen fan—discharge outside.

RAFTERS

IMPROPER VENT

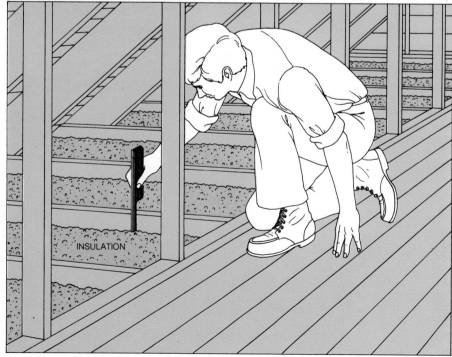

INSULATION

Inspecting the Living Spaces

By correlating visible damage in the finished interior with flaws noted earlier in your inspection—a water-stained ceiling beneath a suspected leak in the attic, for example, or a squeaky floor above sagging joists noted in the basement—you can get a precise idea of what must be done to fix up an old house. During your inspection of the interior you can also estimate the potential expenses of painting and other redecoration, but these are likely to be of less consequence than the cost of essential repairs.

As a rule, if your attic and basement inspections give you a favorable impression, the problems with the interior will be minor. A variety of simple structural and cosmetic repairs, for instance, can restore damaged and squeaky floorboards that might seem hopeless at first glance *(pages 50-55)*, and even substantially damaged plaster on ceilings and walls can be inexpensively replaced with wallboard *(pages 42-43)*.

During your inspection of living quarters, note the type of windows; as a rule wood-framed windows are more energy-efficient and easier to repair than metal-framed windows. Make sure all window locks are secure.

Take time to measure rooms to make sure they will hold your possessions comfortably—empty rooms have a way of looking much larger than they are.

A hard look at wood floors. To check for tilt or sag in a floor, drop a marble or small rubber ball. If it rolls repeatedly and quickly in one direction, indicating sag, inspect the underlying framing for rot *(pages 120-129)*. Throughout the house look for damaged or loose floorboards and check for squeaks or springiness, or for windows rattling as you walk across a floor—all signs of loosened subflooring or poor joist support.

Inspect joints between tongue-and-groove boards: Gaps larger than $1/16$ inch or protruding nailheads make it difficult to sand the floor for refinishing. Also check for a raised lip at hard-to-sand areas—next to the quarter-round shoe molding or under radiators. A lip $1/8$ inch high *(inset)* indicates that the floor has been refinished at least twice and probably cannot be sanded again.

Cracked walls and ceilings. Inspect plaster walls and ceilings for areas of heavy patching and any cracks wider than $1/4$ inch. Wide vertical cracks in a corner, horizontal cracks widening toward the center along the intersection of the ceiling and a partition wall, or large cracks that radiate from doorframes and window frames generally indicate weak or twisted wall framing. If a crack wider than $3/8$ inch crosses the center of a ceiling, look for a visible sag, indicating that the plaster is pulling away from its lath—a condition that requires immediate replastering or patching with gypsum wallboard.

Check wallboard for loosening joint tape or popped-up nails—easy-to-fix cosmetic problems.

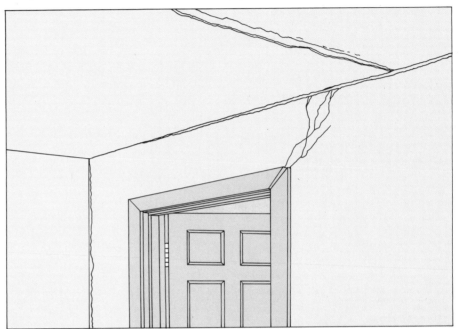

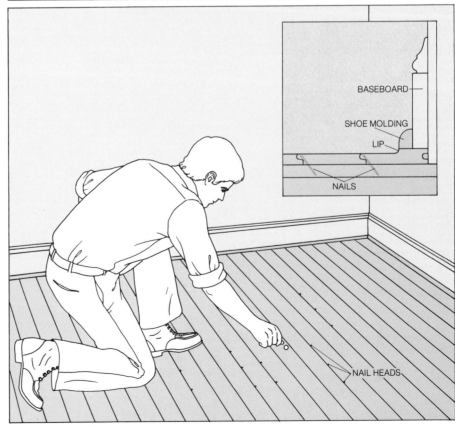

Evaluating the kitchen. Turn on all appliances to make sure they work properly; when checking the stove, test not only the burners on top, but the oven. Check the refrigerator-door seal; cracking and deterioration of the gasket indicate age, but replacing the gasket is easy if you can still find one that will fit. Examine the pipes and the floor under the sink for mold, rust stains or other signs of dampness and leaks. Turn on the faucets full force to see if water pressure is adequate and the hot water is hot.

If you are considering remodeling the kitchen, make sure there is adequate space for new appliances and room for a convenient layout without extensive structural changes. Measure the space around a recessed refrigerator, for instance, to make sure it is large enough for a newer model—probably wider and taller. To install a dishwasher linked to existing plumbing, you need 24 inches of space next to the sink. New overhead cabinets generally require at least 8 to 10 feet of wall space. It is most practical to put a new sink in the same location as the old one, since the plumbing is already there. Look carefully at the flooring for damaged tiles or linoleum that will require replacement.

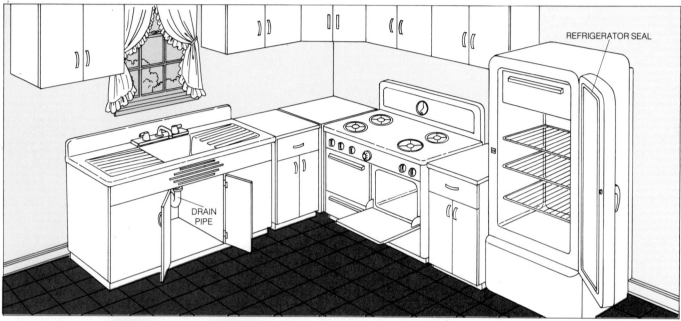

REFRIGERATOR SEAL

DRAIN PIPE

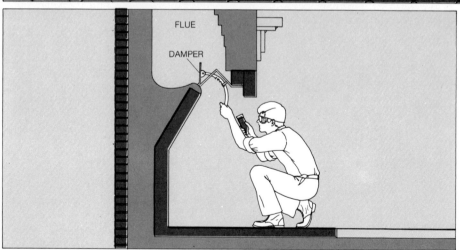

FLUE

DAMPER

SASH CORD

Inspecting fireplaces. Using a flashlight, look for a damper; if there is one, see that it operates easily and closes tightly. Wear goggles to keep soot out of your eyes. With the damper open, examine the flue; the liner should show no crumbling (*pages 68-70*). Inspect the front of the fireplace and the wall above for smoke stains that would indicate poor draw. Measure the flue; it should be about one seventh the area of the fireplace opening, and at least 8 inches by 12 inches for wood fires. Fireplaces that were designed for burning coal and gas have flues too small for wood fires; rebuilding is impractical.

Testing the windows. Check the operation of all windows and look for broken sash cords, rot in wood framing, missing putty and peeling paint. Windows sealed shut by paint are not difficult to free (*pages 56-57*), but if windows are stubborn when there does not seem to be a paint seal, the frames may have settled. Solving this problem is more difficult; you will have to remove and trim the windows.

Also check all doors to see that they operate smoothly and fit precisely in their jambs, and note the quality of the hardware.

The Wiring: Is It Safe?

Since most electrical wiring is hidden inside walls, a complete inspection of all the parts of an electrical system is never possible, but you can determine whether the power supply is adequate, whether the wiring itself is safe for rated loads, and whether the outlets are functional.

Count the wires entering the house from the outside utility poles to find out if there is sufficient voltage. Three wires—two carrying 120 volts each and one neutral wire—provide the standard 240-volt service needed for a modern home. A two-wire, 120-volt system is generally considered inadequate.

If you intend to operate electric appliances such as a clothes dryer, a range or an air conditoner, you will need 100- to 200-ampere capacity, so check the amperage rating on the service panel. This rating is commonly printed on the inside of the door on panels with fuses, or on the main breaker in a panel with circuit breakers—a design typically found in service panels installed since World War II.

Turn off the power (page 83) to a general lighting circuit and remove the cover of an outlet or switch on the deadened circuit to check the condition of wires inside walls; if you find frayed or cracked insulation around the wires there, new wiring is probably needed in various places, although not necessarily throughout the entire house.

Note the number and positions of electrical outlets in each room. If one or two walls in a room have no outlets at all, you will want additional ones installed. Any improvements in the electrical system must meet the requirements of modern building codes, and if you rewire part of the house, there is a possibility that in some locales the inspector may require you to bring the entire house up to electrical-code minimums.

Evaluating a service panel. Power comes to this old 60-ampere panel through a service-entrance cable at the top of the box and is channeled through the main fuse block and the fuses to six house circuits—some of them improperly protected by 30-ampere fuses—that exit from the sides of the box. A bare grounding wire is clamped to a nearby pipe that is at least ¾ inch in diameter—smaller pipes do not provide sufficient grounding.

If the amperage capacity is not listed on a label inside the panel door—or on the main circuit breaker in newer panels—count the fuses to get a rough estimate. A 60-ampere panel has a maximum of eight fuses: if there are more than that, the house almost certainly has at least 100-ampere capacity. Symptoms of circuit overloading include the presence of many 20- and 30-ampere fuses, a burning smell near the panel, fuses whose glass tops are warm to the touch, or darkened and discolored copper contact points under the fuses. Any old panel is probably overloaded by modern appliances; it should be replaced as soon as possible.

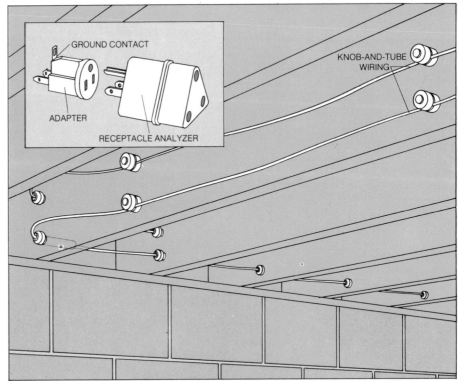

Recognizing worn-out wiring. If joists in the basement are exposed, check the type and condition of wiring runs. If you find the outdated knob-and-tube style shown here, check the wire insulation for any fraying or cracking—these are symptoms that rewiring is urgently needed. Test all of the outlets in the house with a special plug-in receptacle analyzer, adapted when necessary for two-slot outlets (inset). Loosen or remove the outlet-cover screw, attach the adapter's ground wire or contact to this screw and retighten it, then plug in the analyzer. One or more test lights will glow if the outlet is functioning and safely grounded—check the manufacturer's instructions for proper reading of the instrument. If you find ungrounded outlets, consider installing a ground on that circuit—especially for outlets in kitchens and bathrooms.

Plumbing: Is It Free of Clogs?

The original plumbing in an old house usually includes cast-iron drainpipes and either copper or galvanized-steel supply pipes. Cast-iron drainpipes are generally trouble-free for at least 50 years and even then rarely present problems. The copper pipes used widely since about 1935, though they may leak at weak joints, have a life span yet to be determined. But galvanized-steel pipes almost always begin to clog with rust after about 30 years of use. Since they rust from the inside out, by the time rust is visible on the outside they should be replaced. Clogged pipes often cause leaks as well as low water pressure at the faucets.

If the water supply comes from a private well, turn on as many faucets as possible and let them run. If the water becomes muddy within 10 minutes, you probably need a larger storage tank to ensure an adequate water supply. Be sure to have well water tested for purity.

If there is a septic tank for sewage, ask to see the maintenance records. Three- to six-year intervals between pumpings to empty the tank constitute normal maintenance; more frequent pumping implies that the system is inadequate and needs a larger tank. You can often identify the leaching field, where effluence from the septic tank is discharged into the soil, by an area of lush grass in warm months or thin or melted snow in winter. The leaching field should always be on a lower grade than the house. It should never have sections of standing water or mud, or produce an odor of sewage.

Listening for leaks. Locate the main water-supply valve and make sure it works properly. (Some houses have two valves, one on each side of the meter; if this is the case, check both.) If a valve is rusted open, it must be replaced. With the valves open and all the fixtures in the house closed, listen for a gurgling or murmuring sound in a supply pipe—a sign that a leak somewhere in the house is letting the water move. With the valves off, listen for leaking in the supply pipe leading from the street main; if you suspect a leak here, call the water company.

Examining exposed pipes. In the basement, locate the house trap or the cleanout plug for the soil stack and check for scratch marks from tools, indicating frequent removal to remedy clogging. Inspect all visible drains for signs of leaks or patching and look for rust on galvanized-steel supply pipes. Caution: Do not touch such rust spots, as this can break through to cause a leak. If the rust is confined to threaded joints, the pipes are likely to last a few more years, but rust on smooth outside surfaces means that the pipes need to be replaced within a year.

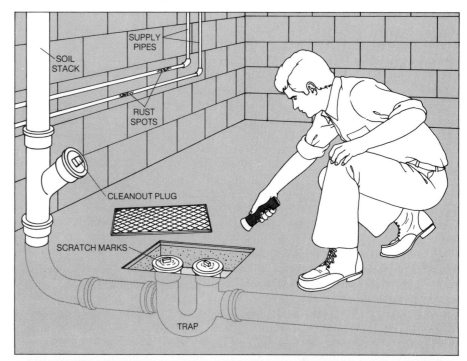

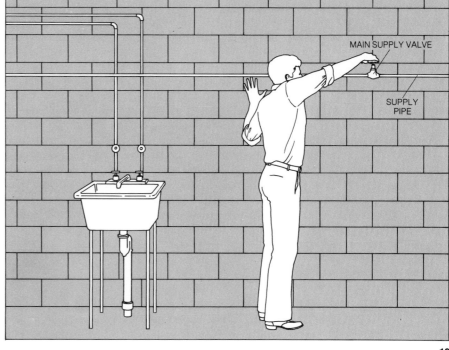

Keeping yourself in hot water. Look for rust or other signs of corrosion on the outside and along the pipes on top of a gas or electric water heater, and examine the floor around the unit for water or water stains—evidence of leaking that tells you the unit should be replaced at once. Open the service door of a gas water heater and look under the burners for rust.

The plate on the outside of the tank will tell you the capacity/recovery rate—how many gallons of hot water the unit holds and how many gallons it will heat in an hour. For a four-person family, a 40/40 rating is usually adequate for a gas water heater—the most common type in old houses. An electric heater, however, should have a capacity half again as great to compensate for its slower recovery rate. On either type of unit, make sure there is a pressure-relief valve: If no valve exists, one must be installed.

Testing the water pressure. In the highest bathroom in the house, turn on the cold-water faucet in the lavatory full force, then do the same with the cold-water faucet in the bathtub. If the flow at the lavatory loses a quarter or more of its original force, rust or corrosion may be starting to clog pipes in supply lines outside or inside. Turn off the cold water and repeat the test with the hot-water faucets; if the water pressure drops again, the hot-water pipes—which run only inside the house—are also becoming clogged. Such partially clogged pipes will probably need replacement in three to five years.

Inspect the caulking, especially around the edge of the tub, and both wall and floor tiles in the bathroom, for deterioration that may permit water damage in rooms below. To prevent such damage, cracked or missing caulking and loose tiles should be replaced as soon as possible.

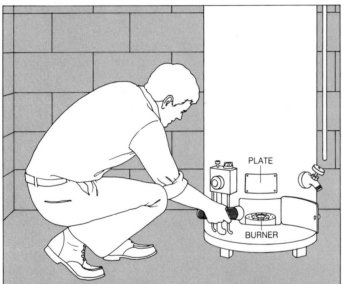

PLATE

BURNER

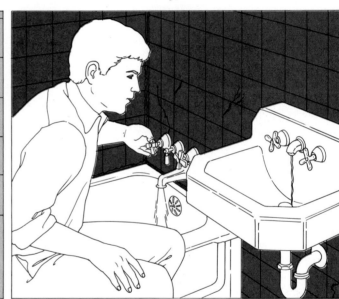

Checking the toilet. Grip the rim of the bowl with both hands and try to wobble it. If it moves at all, there may be a broken seal, which can permit leakage at the base of the bowl. Remove the tank top and look for a date stamped on its underside; this date is frequently a clue to the age of the original plumbing and—since galvanized pipes rarely last more than 50 years—to its probable life expectancy. Inspect the mechanism for corrosion. Flush the toilet to see how long recovery takes before water stops running, and whether there is a strong swirling action in the bowl. Also notice whether the float rod has been bent—a sign that the valve is wearing out and may have to be replaced.

Evaluating the Heating System

Reliable heating is essential in any house, so always conduct a test by turning the furnace on and letting it run for at least 15 minutes—even in midsummer. In an old house, your challenge is to determine whether the system has life left in it, or is nearing its last gasp. Even if a furnace has to be replaced immediately, of course, you face only a calculable expense, not a financial disaster.

Heating systems are defined by the fuel they burn and the way they distribute heat. In most old houses, gas or oil provides the heat, and water or air carries the heat through the house. A water or steam system circulates heat through pipes, a hot-air system through ducts.

A water system is usually more efficient than a hot-air system, since water retains heat longer than air. The water is heated in a boiler, then hot water or steam is circulated—either by a pump or by convection—to room radiators. (Note: Heavy cast-iron radiators retain heat longer than the newer, finned convector units, so a house that has both will not be evenly heated.) Leakage of water from the boiler—usually cast iron with a life span of about 40 years—is the most common cause of failure in this system.

In a hot-air system, air flows over a heat exchanger, enters rooms through supply ducts and is recycled back to the furnace through return ducts. Use your hand to feel for the flow of heat near supply ducts in all finished rooms, and place a tissue near return grilles; suction should hold the tissues against the grilles. The average life of a gas-fired hot-air system in an old house is about 35 years, and the most common cause of failure is a cracked heat exchanger. Cracks in the heat exchanger are dangerous because toxic combustion gases can circulate through the house with the warm air.

An oil-fired boiler. In this heating system, water enters the boiler through supply pipes, is heated by an oil burner, then circulates through the house by convection and gravity flow—hot water rises through the pipes; as it cools, it returns to the boiler. Obvious signs of leaking, such as puddles on the floor and rust stains, sug-gest a worn-out system. Check inside the burner for a heavy deposit of soot—evidence of inefficient combustion—and examine the smoke pipe for rust. To find the installation date, look for an old service tag attached to the boiler or a nearby wall. A unit 40 years old will probably need replacement in a few years.

CIRCULATION PIPES

BURNER

DUCT

FLUE

COMBUSTION CHAMBER

A gas forced-air system. Air is heated in hollow metal heat exchangers (not visible here) mounted in the upper half of this furnace, and is circulated through the house by a blower. Turn the furnace on and remove the upper panel cover. (If you smell a strong odor of gas around an unlit furnace, leave immediately and call the gas company.) After the burners light, hold a match near the flue to test for adequate draw—essential for complete combustion. The flame should bend up into the flue.

When the blower starts, check the flames in the combustion chamber; they should be a distinct blue. Yellow flames indicate incomplete combustion, usually due to dirt-clogged burners. Also watch the flames for wobbling or slanting—a sign that the heat exchanger is cracked and the furnace must be replaced or repaired immediately to prevent toxic gas fumes from leaking into the circulating air. Look for the installation date on a tag on or near the furnace: This type of furnace generally wears out in about 30 years.

How to Find Specialized Professional Help

There are few improvements that a home handyman cannot accomplish with patience and careful planning. Although a professional generally can work faster, a homeowner has the greatest of all incentives to do a job well—he has to live with the results.

If you are like the majority of homeowners, however, you have neither the time nor the tools to do every job yourself. Base your choice of which jobs to undertake on your likes and dislikes. If you are afraid of heights but enjoy painting, hire a roofer and buy your own paintbrushes; someone else who hates painting but loves swinging a hammer on high might do just the opposite. If you take on work you do not enjoy, you will resent the time you spend on it; furthermore, you are likely to take shortcuts and will probably do a sloppy job.

A few jobs should be left to a professional for the sake of safety. You should never attempt to change an electric meter yourself unless you have exceptional skill at wiring. Similarly, the connection of natural-gas piping should be left to a pipe fitter. When you do call for help, you will be able to maintain maximum control and save the most money if you deal directly with the special craftsmen you need—acting, in effect, as your own general contractor.

The directory below—based on the classified pages of the telephone book—lists the most common building trades and services. In each category, you will find information on what these professionals will and will not do and what to look for in a contract with them.

Successful subcontracting depends on careful planning and thorough research. In considering any potential subcontractor, first see that he is reliable. Find out how long he has been in business; if he is new to the trade, try to determine his current credit rating—check for any complaints with a local consumer-protection agency or ask his suppliers whether he pays his bills within a reasonable time. A bankrupt subcontractor can mean heavy losses for you.

Equally important are the quality of a subcontractor's work and his ability to finish work on time. Ask for references from previous clients and, if possible, inspect the workmanship of his past jobs. In many cases you can get sound referrals in your own neighborhood. It is a sign of good performance when a builder can rely on word of mouth to keep him busy in one location.

Whenever possible, secure more than one bid, but make sure you are comparing apples with apples. If materials are included, for instance, make sure your bidders are quoting on materials of comparable quality.

Once you have settled on a subcontractor, draw up a contract. Make rough sketches and spell out—in writing—exactly what work is to be done, specifying the quantities, brand names, grades and model numbers for any materials that are involved. Include a timetable for work and payments and stipulate that the workmen will clean up after the job. Finally, make certain that your subcontractor carries general liability insurance and provides workmen's compensation for himself and his crew.

Architect

A traditional contract with an architect gives him full responsibility for a project and pays him a percentage of the total cost, but for renovation projects it is often possible—and preferable—to find someone who will work at an hourly rate. On this basis, the architect can serve largely as an adviser: He can help you decide what to do, provide drawings and recommend specialists to help. But make sure the architect's tastes and ideas are compatible with your own.

Bricklayer

Often listed under "Mason Contractors" in classified directories, these craftsmen will repoint mortar joints, clean brickwork and repair stucco, and will perform the heavier jobs of building or rebuilding masonry walls, fireplaces and chimneys. Be sure to plan ahead, since bricklayers may be hard to find during times when the weather is good.

Carpenter

The versatility of carpenters makes their skills essential for any renovation work. Some specialize in rough carpentry: framing new walls and floors, reinforcing old, and building forms for concrete. Others do finish carpentry: laying wood floors, hanging doors and installing cabinets and decorative trim. Experienced carpenters are often competent at both. Carpenters work closely with the other trades; they can often recommend other specialists and give you advice on scheduling. While most will use the materials you supply, many get discounts at lumberyards and are willing to pass on the savings to you.

Cement Mason

Check under "Concrete Contractors" or "Paving Contractors" when you want a professional to pour cement—for a slab floor, walls or piers—or to repair a driveway or sidewalk. You may have to make several calls. Many companies are reluctant to do small jobs or give estimates.

Contractor

Generally, you will save time and money dealing directly with subcontractors. But if you have a large number of complicated or interrelated jobs, this middleman may be essential. He will digest the plans, assemble a team of specialists, schedule their work and see that it is executed properly. Some general contractors, particularly those who operate small companies, will allow you to do some of the work yourself to save money. If you take on an intermediate part of a long job, plan to conform to the contractor's schedule. Listings are found under "Contractors—General."

Dry-Wall Man

Any careful amateur can install small pieces of dry wall, but large sheets are unwieldy and, unless you have a helper, subcontracting this work may be the best way to guarantee a neat job. Many general carpenters will do this work, but check directory listings under "Dry Wall Contractors" as well.

Electrician

Whenever you call in an electrician, you can reasonably expect that any job will be done to professional standards. In most areas an electrician must pass a licensing examination, and electrical work must be inspected after the rough wiring is in and again after the job is completed. Most electricians will take small jobs or completely rewire an old house.

Excavating Contractor

This subcontractor has the heavy equipment to do grading, trenching or backfilling around a house, or even to excavate a basement or swimming pool. It may be difficult to find one willing to take a small grading job, so also try listings under "Paving Contractors" and "Landscape Contractors." The latter prefer jobs in which they can sell you some trees, plants or sod, but they are equipped to do grading around houses.

Exterminator

Most exterminators will contract for a single job or for ongoing services with a renewable guarantee. The market is competitive; shop around for the best price.

Floor Layer

Professional floor layers work with carpeting, linoleum and tile floor coverings and may specialize in one of these. Usually floor layers supply materials and labor; check the quality and price of materials as well as workmanship. This service is sometimes available through department stores, but look also under "Floor Laying, Refinishing and Resurfacing," "Carpet Layers" and "Linoleum Layers."

Floor Sander and Refinisher

For specialists who refinish wood floors, look under "Floor Laying, Refinishing and Resurfacing." Try carpenters as well. Always postpone floor refinishing until all your messy jobs have been finished.

Glazier

Contract with a glazier—often listed under "Glass" in the directory—to cut, fit and install insulating glass or plate-glass windows, mirrors and glass doors. Glaziers generally will provide both materials and labor.

Heating and Cooling Contractors

Look for listings under "Heating Contractors" for work on either a furnace or air conditioner. Most companies feature a specific brand of appliance, so first determine the most appropriate unit for your needs. Generally, the contractor provides all the equipment and oversees his own crew of specialists—sheet-metal workers for air ducts, licensed plumbers or electricians for final connections. For repair jobs, make sure to ascertain the minimum charge for a service call as well as the hourly rates.

Insulation Worker

Insulation materials come in a variety of forms—rolls, sheets, pellets, blocks and pastes—and some contractors specialize in only one or two. In many areas the home-insulation business has become a very competitive market. Get several bids and familiarize yourself with the type, insulating value and fire rating of the material each salesman is promoting.

Ornamental-Iron Worker

Telephone listings for ornamental-iron workers are usually mixed with heavy-industry listings under "Iron Works." These craftsmen can fabricate and install, or repair, metal balconies, gates, fences, stairways, window grilles and the like.

Painter and Paperhanger

Some professionals do both, but painting and paperhanging are often considered separate trades. Most of the cost of either goes for labor, so shop for the best rate you can get for quality work. A local subcontractor recommended by your neighbors is often the best bet unless you need exterior painting that requires scaffolding. In that case you may want a larger firm, listed under "Painting Contractors" or "Wall Coverings."

Plasterer and Lather

Because most interior-wall finishing is now done with gypsum wallboard, locating a plasterer for interior walls, exterior stucco or ornamental moldings may call for some detective work. Check the listings under "Plastering Contractors." Ask local carpenters, general contractors or the managers of old apartment buildings for recommendations. Call a plasterer as far in advance as possible.

Plumber

Plumbing work, like electrical work, is regulated by code and licensing requirements. The plumber assembles and maintains any piping that carries water, steam or gas. He can also install and connect household appliances, such as a water heater or dishwasher. Look for listings under "Plumbing Contractors."

Roofer

A roofer resurfaces or repairs the outer layer of a roof to ensure that it is watertight; some will work on the underlying structure while others employ carpenters to replace sheathing or rafters. Select a recommended roofer specializing in your type of surface—asphalt, slate, tile, wood shingles, tin. Insist on a guarantee for a new roof; try to get one for any repair work as well. Many roofers repair gutters and will waterproof walls and basements. Some department stores contract for roofing and gutter work; also check listings under "Roofing Contractors."

Septic-Tank Serviceman

These specialists pump out and clean septic tanks. They often offer sewer- and drain-cleaning services as well. Septic-tank servicing is available in most areas, for a single job or as a continuing service.

Stonemason

This craftsman works with stone as a structural material in walls and chimneys and as a decorative surface for floors, patios and stairs. Look for classified listings under the heading "Mason Contractors." You may have to make several calls to find a stonemason willing to do a small repair job.

2

Casting a plaster molding. A rubber mold is peeled away to expose the hardened plaster cast beneath. The mold—a perfect reproduction, but in reverse—is made by pouring liquid rubber around a good section of molding. When the rubber has hardened, it can be used again and again to recreate sections of elaborate trim.

The face of American residential architecture has changed dramatically through the years, but America's infatuation with gewgaws and fancy woodwork has been surprisingly persistent. Georgian houses of the 18th Century were full of carved paneling, decorated doorways, elaborate mantels and exquisitely turned stair rails. The Federal house, a product of the early 19th Century, was decorated inside and out with eagles, cornucopias, lions and lyres made of wood, brass and stone. Turn-of-the-century row houses and mansions, loosely called Victorian, held a smorgasbord of decorative moldings, carvings, hardware and stained glass borrowed from every preceding era.

Unfortunately, the ornaments that delighted the homeowners of yesteryear are today often damaged or hidden. The challenge to a new owner is to peel away the paint and linoleum of countless remodelings and polish up the age-worn parts that make an old house unique. Once the essential repairs are taken care of, from fixing roofs to unsticking windows, you can put away the hammers, saws and trowels and become a detective, a cannibal and a mixer of magic potions.

An old house may be filled with buried treasures waiting to be discovered by a homeowner with patience and persistence. Scrape away enough wall paint and you may reveal the remains of the original wallpaper so you can come close to duplicating its design. With a sensitive hand or a careful eye, you may detect under wall paint the ever-so-slight ripples of a stenciled frieze. But many charming details will be right before your eyes, and even if their original purposes are obscure, they are almost always worth adapting to modern use. For example, a niche carved into the wall at the curve of a stairway, originally constructed so it would be possible to maneuver cumbersome pieces of furniture up and down the stairs, may now provide a perfect place to display flowers.

Fixing up old treasures requires as much ingenuity as finding them. No store-bought wood stain can enhance a mahogany molding quite as well as the colors you concoct yourself with ground pigment, turpentine and linseed oil. You cannot glue shattered bits of marble back to the edge of a mantel shelf, but you can fill the chip with a potion that looks pretty much like the real thing. And if a section of elaborate old wood molding needs to be replaced, you can duplicate its profile with shaped blades fitted on a table saw.

When nothing else will work, you can resort to constructive cannibalizing. To replace a cracked floorboard in the middle of the dining room, pilfer a matching board from inside a closet. To duplicate the ornate detail of a cast-plaster molding, steal its design from a good section, then cast a new piece.

Restoring Fine Details: Locks, Knobs, Ironwork

Stained-glass windows, antique brass escutcheons and old-fashioned surface-mounted door locks are only a few of the charming accouterments that adorn old houses and set them apart from their modern neighbors. These fixtures and others such as wrought-iron railings and marble mantels often need only small repairs and cleaning to transform them from shoddy to shiny. Such small fixes not only embellish the house, but in some cases—stiffening a loose railing, for example—are imperative for safety.

Sometimes, of course, you may have to live with imperfections. Turn-of-the-century imported stained glass with ripples, streaks and bubbles may be so difficult to duplicate that living with a crack is better than replacing the piece with a modern mismatch. A marble mantel with a major crack calls for the advice of an expert in the intricacies of stone joinery.

Loose iron railings are another matter, since they make outdoor steps unsafe. The repair illustrated on page 29 tightens a wobbling rail by adding a metal sleeve—round and square ones are available at ironworks—to the bottom of a post weakened by rust. Along the top, a cap rail loose from its lower U-shaped channel can be fastened down with aluminum rivets from a hardware store. More complicated railing repairs—the mending or replacement of broken or missing parts—generally call for skill in handling welding equipment and other metal-working tools.

Even a sturdy railing is likely to need refinishing, not for looks alone but to stop the ravages of rust. Scrape off old paint and all rust (opposite, bottom), then brush on a rust-resistant primer coat of zinc chromate and one or two coats of enamel formulated for exterior metal.

The metal inside an old house can also be damaged by rust. Surface-mounted door locks, usually made of cast iron, are especially susceptible. An old and rusted exterior door lock should be replaced with a newer model for the sake of security, but a sluggish interior lock, once cleaned and lubricated, should work like new if all of its parts are intact. Although there are as many different designs as there were companies making these locks, the basic configuration is similar to that of the two locks below.

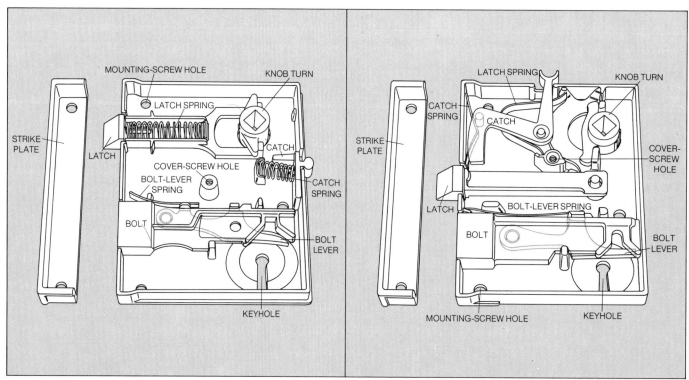

Two interior rim locks. The two locks illustrated here are mounted so that their strike plates are on the rim of the jamb and their bodies on the door face. For cleaning or repairing, first remove the knob, then remove the lock body from the door by removing the mounting screws. Set the lock on a flat surface and, with a cloth covering your hand and the lock to catch springs that may pop out, unscrew the central screw that holds the cover in place.

Use tweezers to lift out large dust particles, then check for broken, misaligned or missing parts. Each of the locks has three springs, flat or coiled. One spring presses against the bolt lever; turning the door key pushes up the spring and simultaneously moves the bolt in or out. A latch spring holds the latch extended. A catch spring provides the tension for a small catch that can lock the latch in place. Have a locksmith replace any broken or missing springs. Other metal

parts may be more difficult to replace or repair. A bent bolt can sometimes be straightened in a vise, but the force may break the bolt.

Before you start cleaning the parts, sketch or photograph the lock. If you have two, leave one assembled as a model. Then remove all the parts. Bathe them in paint stripper, grease them with a lock-lubricating solution available from a locksmith and replace them in the lock.

Quick Fixes for Porcelain Knobs

Tightening and cleaning a knob. To secure a porcelain knob that is loose on its metal stem, use a toothpick to force a small amount of epoxy glue into the joint between the porcelain and the stem. If the bolts that hold the knob to the projecting cam are missing or are so worn that they allow the knob to wobble, replace them with new bolts of the same size.

Remove paint from a porcelain knob by covering the surrounding metal with masking tape, then wiping the knob with a water-rinsing paint stripper (*page 34*). Buff the knob with a porcelain-polishing compound, which can be bought in paste form at hardware stores. Cover small chips and cracks with porcelain paint, which is available in hardware stores.

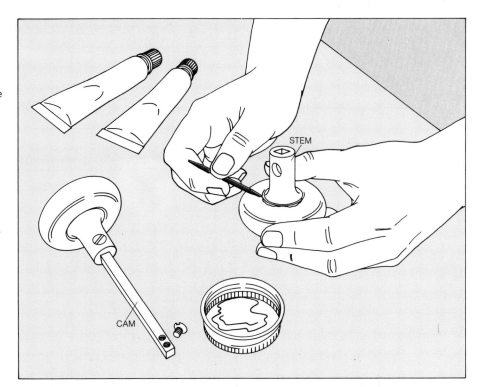

Stripping a Flaking Iron Railing

Burning off old paint. With a flame-spreader accessory attached to the nozzle of a propane torch, direct the flame against a section of rail until the paint begins to blister. Always hold the torch upright and direct the flame away from you; always wear a respirator. Point the flame away from the rail and remove the softened paint with a scraper. Heat and scrape the rest of the paint. For areas where the scraper cannot reach, use an electric drill with a wire-brush attachment, a hand-held wire brush or a water-rinsing paint stripper. Caution: Never use the torch after applying paint stripper.

Remove any rust you find under the paint with a liquid rust remover, then apply zinc chromate primer and one or two coats of paint.

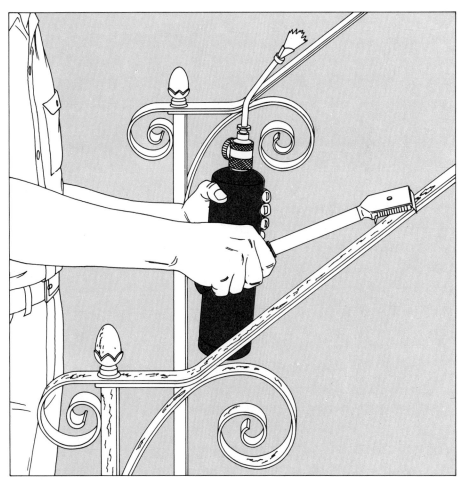

Anchoring a Loose Railing Cap

1 Drilling the rail. To help straighten a warped iron stair-rail cap and to secure it to the U-shaped channel beneath it *(inset)*, drill a $5/16$-inch hole through both the cap and the channel. First use a center punch and hammer to make a small indentation that will guide the drill bit to an accurate start. After the hole is drilled, enlarge its top end with a countersink bit.

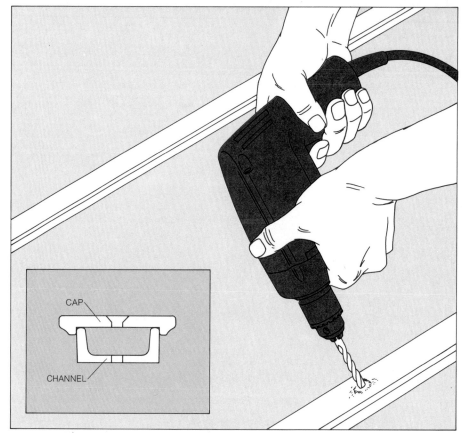

2 Joining with a rivet. Slide a ¼-inch aluminum rivet up through the drilled hole, using a rivet that protrudes ¼ inch above the top of the cap. Support the rivet under the channel with the poll (flat face) of a ball-peen or claw hammer and use the peen (rounded face) of a ball-peen hammer to flatten the end of the rivet into the countersunk hole in the cap. There should be no projection above the surface of the rail.

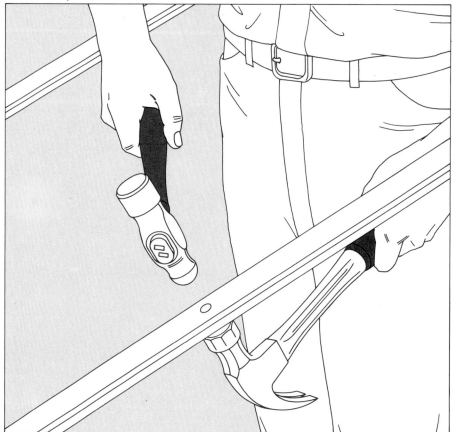

Resetting a Rail Post

1 Digging out and reinforcing posts. If the bottom ends of loose posts on an iron stair rail are not loose enough to be uprooted by hand, chip away the surrounding brick or concrete with a flat-bladed cold chisel and a ball-peen hammer. Wear goggles. Remove the entire rail, then enlarge the postholes until they are 1 inch wider than the posts and 5 inches deep.

Clean the post ends with a liquid rust remover, then use a hacksaw to cut a 10-inch steel sleeve for each post—round for round posts, square for square ones.

If the tip of a post has deteriorated with rust, cut off enough to reach solid metal, then add the number of inches you cut off to the length of the new sleeve. Slip a sleeve over each post end so that the sleeve overlaps the post by 5 inches.

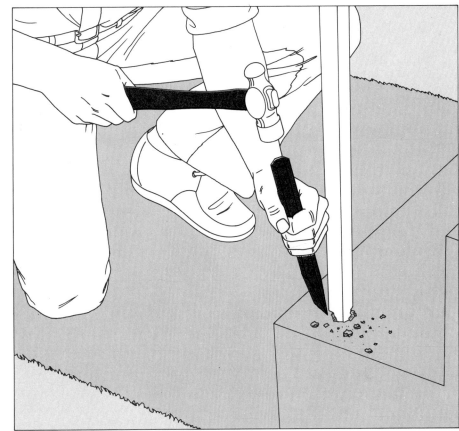

2 Securing the sleeves. Drill two $5/16$-inch holes through each sleeve and post, then insert a $1/4$-inch stove bolt through each and tighten with a screwdriver and wrench. Cover the joint between the sleeve and post with metal filler, available in tubes at hardware stores, to keep the inside of the sleeve dry.

Set the posts in the prepared holes; plumb the railing with a level and brace it in place with 2-by-4s wedged into the ground on one side of the stair. Mix a small amount of concrete and pour it into the holes; slope the concrete slightly so that it will shed water. If you are setting the posts in brick, add brick dust to the concrete to match the brick color. Leave the braces in place overnight while the concrete hardens.

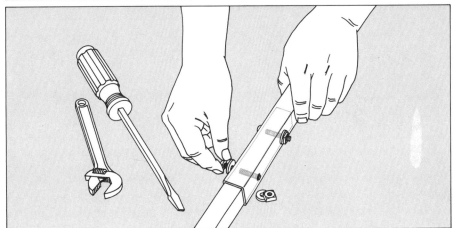

Cleaning and Polishing Brass

Unlike iron, brass does not rust, but without regular polishing it will tarnish. Light tarnish can be removed with an ordinary commercial brass cleaner, but for heavy tarnish, follow these steps:
□ Dissolve the tarnish by soaking the brass in a plastic container holding a mixture of ½ pint of vinegar, 4 table- spoons of salt and a quart of water. Wear rubber gloves; these ingredients make dilute hydrochloric acid. Let the brass soak in the solution overnight.
□ With the tarnish removed, use a paste polish and a soft cloth, or an electric drill with a buffing attachment, to shine the brass.

□ To slow further tarnishing, use a clear, spray-on acrylic coating. Apply three coats, letting each one dry for two hours. This should prevent tarnish for several years. When tarnish reappears, strip the acrylic with any commercial paint remover, repolish the brass and reapply the acrylic.

The Fragile Beauty of Marble and Stained Glass

Marble mantels and leaded stained-glass windows lend an air of elegance to an old house. But marble and glass are fragile, and the passing years take their toll in cracks, chips, stains and sags. Often, only minor repairs are needed. Cracked or broken pieces of stained glass can be replaced with colored glass available in hobby shops. You can remove stains from marble either by washing or by applying a cleansing poultice; you can fill cracks or chips in marble with an epoxy mixture colored to match the marble.

Before beginning any marble repair, however, be sure you are really working with marble. In the 19th Century, many mantels were made of dark-gray soapstone, cast iron or wood, then marbleized—painted to look like the real thing. The best way to uncover such old-time trompe l'oeil work is to examine the back of a piece—scratch it if necessary—to see if the face color and graining are continuous. If they are not, do not use any of the repair or cleansing techniques discussed here—only a professional can touch up and restore these mantels.

Similarly, repairing severe cracks or breaks in a real-marble mantel calls for the skill of an expert stoneworker who can disassemble the mantel, glue the pieces together, then reinforce the stone with steel bars. But a small chip on any horizontal marble surface can be filled almost invisibly with an epoxy mixture. All the supplies are found in hardware stores: a two-part epoxy glue (1 part resin, 1 part hardener), painter's whiting, and dry powdered mineral pigments.

To make the epoxy filler, pour enough whiting into the epoxy resin to form a thick paste. Add pigment, then hardener according to directions, and use the filler immediately. (Before mixing a large batch, mix a small amount, keeping track of the proportions, and test the filler on a scrap of wood to be sure the color is right.) After the patch in the marble has hardened and has been sanded smooth, use nonyellowing paste wax to polish it.

A cracked piece of stained glass can also be repaired with glue—a clear epoxy spread over a crack may be enough to prevent further damage. When it is not, replace the glass (pages 32-33).

To work with glass, you need several tools—all readily available. For scoring the glass before breaking it, use a glass cutter with a ball on the end of the handle; for final shaping and fitting, you may need a pair of grozing pliers. Use a lead knife to cut the lead channels, called came, that hold the individual pieces of glass in the window. And for setting new pieces of glass in place, use an 80-watt soldering iron and wire solder that is 50 per cent tin and 50 per cent lead.

Wear goggles when cutting glass and work in a well-ventilated area—fumes are given off by the kerosene needed to lubricate the glass-cutter wheel and by the liquid flux (either oleic acid or zinc chloride) used with the solder. Gloves are optional—experts never use them because they are awkward and slippery. If you choose not to wear gloves, work slowly and carefully—some of the glass edges will be razor-sharp. Clear the table frequently of all glass fragments.

Fortunately, the easiest and most common stained-glass repairs do not require glass cutting. Leaded-glass windows have a tendency to bow in time because the soft lead contracts and expands with temperature changes. If a window is bowed more than 1 inch, take it to an expert for restructuring, but if it is less severely bowed, try weighting it with books—adding one average-sized book every hour—to flatten it. After the window is flattened, strips of thin steel soldered to the came across the less important side—usually the outside—will prevent future bowing.

If sections of glass rattle because the lead channels are no longer snug around them, you can mix a filler that will eliminate the rattle and clean the glass and lead at the same time. Mix 1 cup of turpentine with 1 cup of linseed oil and, wearing a respirator, add plaster of paris until the mixture has the consistency of pancake batter. Stir in lampblack or India ink until the filler is dark gray. Use the mixture as directed at the bottom of the opposite page.

Cleaning Stained Marble

Marble fixtures that are in good condition are best maintained by regular washing with a mild detergent. You can repolish a small area of marble with tin oxide powder, available from stone dealers (a large job requires the special tools and skill of an expert). Wet the marble, sprinkle with powder and buff vigorously with a buffing pad attached to an electric drill.

Several hard-to-remove stains that require more than a household cleaner can be erased from marble with the use of a poultice—a paste of powdered painter's whiting and a liquid chemical dictated by the nature of the stain. This paste is spread ½ inch thick over the stain and kept moist for 48 hours under plastic kitchen wrap secured with masking tape. To finish, scrape off the paste with a putty knife and rinse the marble clean with water.

Organic stains are caused by tea, coffee, ink, burning tobacco, soft drinks, fruit juices, flowers and colored paper or fabric. They usually take the shape of the object that caused them—the bottom of a coffee cup, for instance. Make the poultice of 80 per cent whiting, 20 per cent hydrogen peroxide and a few drops of ammonia.

Other organic stains are caused by fatty or greasy substances—milk, butter, hand lotion or peanut butter, for example. Use a poultice of whiting with enough acetone added to form a thick paste; acetone, most familiar as nail-polish remover, is readily available at cosmetics counters.

Rust stains are orange to brown and generally take the shape of the metal object that caused them. If you are unable to remove such a stain by rubbing it vigorously with a dry cloth, make a poultice of powdered household cleanser and water.

To remove soot and smoke stains from a marble mantel, use a poultice of baking soda and liquid bleach.

Epoxy Filler for an Invisible Patch

1 **Filling in the chip.** Use a heat gun *(page 36)* or hair dryer to dry the damaged area thoroughly, then stick masking tape around the damaged place to make a form slightly wider and deeper than the missing piece. Pour the tinted epoxy mixture *(opposite)* into the form until the mixture is slightly higher than the marble. Let the epoxy dry overnight, then remove the tape.

Simulating marble graining, a job that requires a steady hand, should be done before the epoxy dries. Dip a fine-tipped paintbrush in powdered pigment and brush streaks onto the new piece while the epoxy is still sticky.

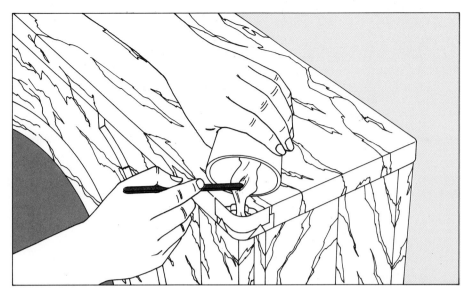

2 **Sanding the epoxy.** Misting the surrounding marble with water to prevent scratching, use fine-grit, wet-type sandpaper to smooth the epoxy patch with firm circular strokes. Sand the epoxy until it is level with the marble.

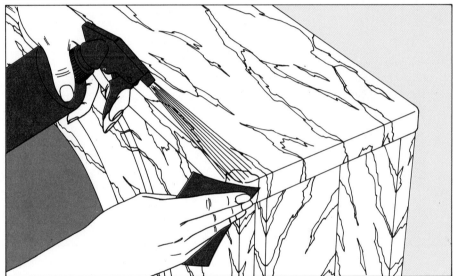

Silencing a Window Rattle

Spreading the filler. With the window flat on a table, scoop up a handful of filler mixed as described opposite and spread it over the entire window, pushing it between the lead and the glass *(inset)* with your fingertips. (Wear rubber gloves and a respirator.) Sprinkle plaster of paris over the wet filler mixture and scrub both glass and lead with a stiff-bristled brush. Wipe away the excess filler and plaster with a dry cloth. Turn the window over and repeat the process.

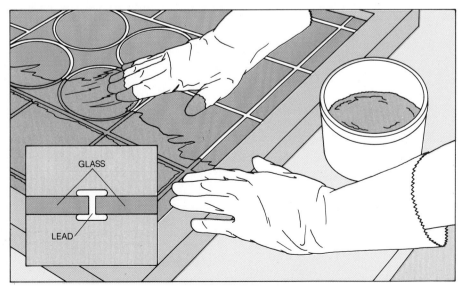

GLASS

LEAD

Replacing Cracked Glass

1 **Breaking out the damaged piece.** Lay the window flat with the smoother side of the stained glass facing up and a wooden support block under the cracked glass. Make several crisscrossing scores across the cracked piece, dipping the cutter in kerosene for each score to avoid dulling the wheel. To make the scores, hold the cutter between your index and middle fingers; then, keeping your wrist locked and applying firm downward pressure, draw the cutter toward you in a continuous motion.

Set the window on edge, scores facing away from you, and use the ball on the cutter handle to rap the glass firmly until it breaks out of the lead.

2 **Cutting away the old lead.** Decide which side of the window is looked at less, lay the window with that side up and, around the open area, use a lead knife to shave away the upper flange of the H-shaped came down to the crosspiece (*inset*). Rub the lead lightly with steel wool so the solder to be applied later will adhere.

Set the new piece of stained glass over the open area and use a thin-line felt-tipped pen to trace on the new glass an outline of the inside edge of the lead visible below. If the glass is so dark you cannot see the lead, trace a pattern on clear, stiff plastic and cut it out with scissors. Then outline the pattern on the new glass.

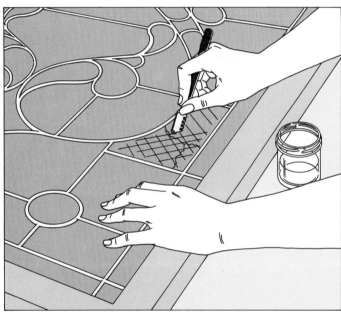

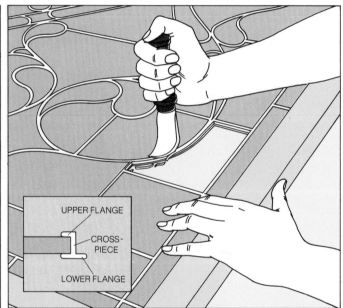

UPPER FLANGE

CROSS-
PIECE

LOWER FLANGE

3 **Cutting the new piece.** Working on top of several sheets of newspaper spread over a worktable, score a straight part of the outline from one edge of the glass to the other with a single stroke. Use a ruler if you need a guide for the cutter. Snap off the waste glass by placing your thumbs on top of the glass on either side of the score, making a fist with each hand below the glass, and twisting your wrists so that your thumbs press outward to snap the glass along the score. To cut curves, make a few gently curved scores outside the guideline (*inset*) and snap off the outer sections one at a time.

If the glass does not snap easily, lift it and tap along the underside of the score with the ball end of the glass cutter until the score becomes a visible fracture, then snap the glass. If you are working with a piece of glass that is too large for you to pick up, start by making straight scores and snapping them over the edge of the table.

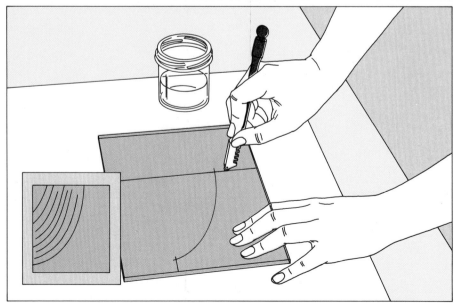

4 Grozing for a perfect fit. The new piece should slip easily into its place in the window but if it does not, note where it binds. Use the tips of a pair of grozing pliers to nibble away bits of glass, no more than $1/16$ inch at a time. Then set the fitted piece back in the window.

5 Rebuilding the flange. To replace the cut-away lead flange with a strip of solder, use a small brush to apply flux to the exposed lead crosspiece all around the new glass, then uncoil 5 inches of solder. Prepare the soldering iron by coating its tip with a thin layer of solder for the most effective heat diffusion. Touch the tip of the iron to the end of the uncoiled length of solder wherever you want to start the solder strip. As the solder melts onto the lead and glass, creating a new flange, keep the iron moving—if you stop, the heat may crack the glass. Set the hot iron down only on an abestos pad or in a holder. Excess solder that gets onto the glass can be cut away when cold. Clean the tip of the iron often by wiping it quickly across a damp sponge.

After soldering the new glass, cement it as shown on page 31, at the same time filling in any loose spots along the came of the entire window.

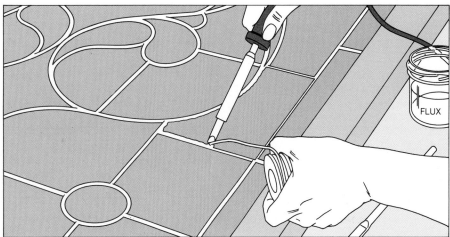

Reinforcing a Bowed Window

1 Drilling holes in the frame. Set the bowed window on a flat surface with the convex side facing up. Then, for the ends of flat steel reinforcement strips, drill $1/4$-inch holes $1/4$ inch deep in the inside edges of the frame. Flatten the bowed area by gradually weighting it down with books, or, if the bowing is not severe, by pressing on it with both hands. Caution: Excessive pressure may crack the glass. Cut $1/8$-inch steel into $1/4$-inch-wide strips, as long as the width of the window plus $1/2$ inch; use at least three parallel strips, more for a large window.

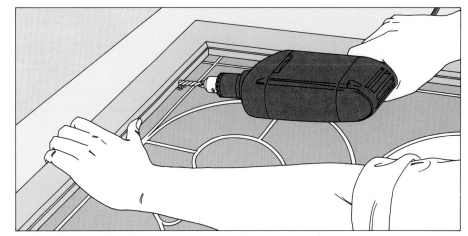

2 Soldering the reinforcement bar. Bend each reinforcement strip enough to fit it, narrow edge up, into the drilled holes, then apply flux to each place the strip crosses lead. Drip enough solder at each intersection to join the lead and steel.

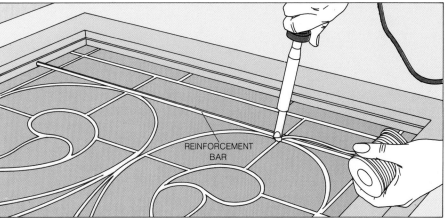

REINFORCEMENT BAR

Rescuing the Elegance of Old Wood Trim

In some old houses the moldings were the signature of the builder. They were painstakingly shaped with hand planes to elaborate contours, and made from fine hardwoods—mahogany, walnut, ash or cherry—that would be prohibitively expensive today. But the trim in most old houses is in poor condition, with surfaces dulled or shapes concealed under layers of paint. The obvious solution is to cut back or strip away the old finishes, then finish the wood anew.

The work of stripping an old finish varies tremendously with the nature of the finish. If your woodwork is stained and varnished and the finish has darkened with age, you may need only to clean it to reveal the wood-grain pattern. Start with turpentine or mineral spirits to remove wax and grime; then, if necessary, use strong cleansers, such as trisodium phosphate, ammonia or washing soda. Denatured alcohol (methyl hydrate) and lacquer thinner can also be used to clean varnish, but the first dissolves shellac and the second, lacquer, so they should be tried carefully. Turpentine or mineral spirits will clean lacquer and shellac. Caution: All of these can harm eyes and skin; wear rubber gloves and goggles.

Unfortunately, a more difficult job—stripping painted wood clean of all or part of its finish—is the one that is in most cases necessary: Most old moldings are covered by layers of paint. One recourse is to remove the trim from the walls and take it to a professional, who will soak it clean in a special chemical bath. But removing old and fragile wood is risky. Probably you will have to strip the wood in place—a job that can call for hours of messy work.

There are several ways to remove the paint. It can be loosened with a stripper—a chemical solvent that softens the paint and destroys its bond to a wood surface—and then scraped off with a putty knife or a special molding scraper; or it can be softened with a heating iron (which heats the air above the paint) or a heat gun (which blows hot air against it) and then scraped away.

All chemicals strong enough to remove paint involve certain hazards and must be selected and used with great care. The best strippers for indoor work are made with methylene chloride. Though they are the most expensive, they are non-flammable; they also are very effective on oil-base paints. They are not as effective, however, on latex-base paint, the water-thinned finish that has been the most common since World War II.

To cut through latex you will need a stripper that contains methanol, toluol and acetone. These chemicals, whether or not combined with methylene chloride as they sometimes are, are highly flammable. When using them, keep away all flames or cigarettes, turn off any pilot lights in the room and keep your solvent-soaked work pad away from electrical outlets. When using any stripper, open the doors and windows wide and protect your skin with rubber gloves.

Some strippers are sold in both liquid and pastelike forms. For convenience, choose the semipaste version: It contains a complex wax that helps it adhere to vertical surfaces. Strippers contain active solvents that must be chemically neutralized on the wood after the stripper has done its work. To simplify this part of the job, choose a product labeled "water rinsing"; the solvents in such a stripper can be neutralized with trisodium phosphate and hot water.

Before you strip large sections of trim, use some stripper and a sharp scraping tool to clean thoroughly a small patch of wood, and consider both the difficulty of this small job and the quality of the wood you expose. Only a fine-grained hardwood warrants the labor of full-fledged stripping, down to the bare wood. Many old softwood moldings may have lovely shapes but undistinguished grains. These moldings were intended to be painted, and they are best repainted now. If their details have been obscured by many coats of paint, you must do some stripping, using dropcloths to protect the floor, but you can stop well short of totally stripping the wood.

Begin such a partial stripping job with a heat gun or heating iron; when you have removed enough layers of old paint to reveal the detail of the molding, use a chemical stripper to smooth the surface for repainting. If you do uncover hardwood and decide to strip the wood bare, start right in with stripping chemicals and use them generously, to clean out the pores of the wood.

A fully stripped molding must be refinished to protect the newly bared surface and to show off the natural beauty of the wood. The finish coatings for fine woodwork listed on the chart at the top of the opposite page are all easy to apply; the crucial—and relatively tedious—part of the refinishing job is preparing the wood for the finish.

Sand the wood lightly by hand—the smoother and cleaner the surface, the better the new finish will look. Sanding will smooth out any wood fibers that rise from the surface when you rinse off the stripping chemicals, and will remove some dark patches on bare wood, generally water stains. But most of these stains run deep into the wood and must be lightened with oxalic acid or common laundry bleach. Spot bleaching may suffice, but generally you will have to bleach the whole piece, using a pad of fine steel wool to rub bleach over the surface. Apply the bleach repeatedly until the spots disappear, then sand again.

When you complete this job and have the wood stripped and bleached, its appearance may surprise you. Raw walnut is not dark brown but has a grayish cast; raw mahogany is not a rich, deep red but ranges from brown to tan. Some people prefer this truly natural appearance, and if you do, finishing requires only the application of shellac, varnish or wax. But this obviously will not restore the original look of trim in an old house. When such woods were used for trim moldings—mainly between the Civil War and World War I—they were stained to give the familiar deep colors and to enrich the appearance of the grain patterns.

Stains, available in many shades, are simply brushed or wiped on. The best commercial stains are penetrating oils, which seep into the wood and do not conceal the grain. If you need to match the color of unstripped molding, mix your own stain. Experiment with pigments ground in oil in these shades: burnt umber, burnt sienna, raw umber and raw sienna. Mix the pigments with turpentine until you get the right shade, then add 4 tablespoons of japan drier for each ½ pint of stain.

A Stripper or Cleanser for Every Job

Stripping Agent	Use	Remarks
FULL STRIPPERS		
Methylene chloride removers	Effective on lacquers, varnishes, polyurethane, oil-based paints and thin layers of latex paint	Nonflammable, expensive
Methanol, toluol, acetone mix	Removes heavy layers of latex-based and oil-based paints, lacquer and varnishes	Flammable, use indoors with special caution
PARTIAL STRIPPERS AND CLEANERS		
Denatured alcohol	Dissolves shellac	Can be diluted with lacquer thinner to cut back rather than remove the finish
Trisodium phosphate and ammoniated household cleansers	Partially removes shellac and varnish	Can be diluted with hot water to vary their strengths
Heat gun or heating iron	Removes built-up paint layers	Useful when wood is to be repainted; will not fully clean wood surface; requires some chemical cleanup

Choosing the right stripper. Use this chart after determining the quality and condition of the wood in your trim. If you wish to strip fine hardwood bare, use a full stripper, chosen from the first two stripping agents in the first column of the chart. If you plan to retain a stained or painted finish, choose a cleaner or a partial stripper from the last three agents. The second column of the chart indicates the specific finishes best removed by each stripper; the third deals with their applications and limitations.

Finishes for Protection and Beauty

Finish	Durability	Moisture Resistance	Appearance	Remarks
HARD FINISHES				
Shellac	Fair	Poor	Available with a clear base or with a slight orange tint; polishes well to a high gloss; darkens with age	Easy to touch up or to strip; dissolves in alcohol; do not use as a finish around a bar
Alkyd resin varnish	Good	Good when mixed with tung oil, poor with other oils	Clear; can be rubbed to add luster	Recoats easily; cannot be used over shellac, linseed oil or polyurethane
Polyurethane varnish	Excellent	Excellent	Dries to a very high gloss; becomes cloudy with heavy wear; objectionable to some woodworkers for its synthetic appearance	Must be roughened before recoating; generally incompatible with other finishes
OIL FINISHES				
Boiled linseed	Poor	Poor	Prized for its soft sheen	Recoats easily, coats other finishes well; poor base for shellac or polyurethane
Rubbing and antiquing	Good	Fair	Can be rubbed to varying degrees of clarity or gloss	Excellent as a finishing coat, except over shellac
Tung	Good	Good	Normally a matte finish but can be thinned and buffed to a shine; wrinkles in heavy coats	Not compatible with shellac; easy to refinish

Choosing the right finish. The first column of this chart lists the most commonly used clear finishes for wood trim, grouped in two categories: relatively hard finishes, which stand up well to wear; and relatively soft oil finishes, valued mainly for their appearance. If the wood is subject to heavy use, as in a chair rail or door casing, or may be exposed to liquids or high humidity, give special weight to the durability of the finish (Column 2) and its resistance to moisture (Column 3); if the wood is primarily decorative, make the clarity, gloss and tone of a finish (Column 4) the primary considerations. The fifth column of the chart deals with special problems of application and maintenance.

Working with Chemical Strippers

1 **Applying the stripper.** Having provided good ventilation and wearing rubber gloves, brush stripper onto the wood with short strokes in one direction—back-and-forth brushwork damages the chemical's bond with the finish. Let the stripper stand for 20 minutes, until the paint liquifies into a sludge, then scrape the wood clean with a wide-bladed putty knife whose sharp corners have been filed round. The sludge should come off the wood in a continuous ribbon; if it does not, brush on another coat of the stripper and wait for a few more minutes before scraping.

2 **Cleaning contours.** For grooves and corners that cannot be reached with a wide-bladed putty knife, choose a scraping tool with a contour as close as possible to the contour you must clean. A molding scraper, which has interchangeable blades to fit most common molding shapes, is one choice. A cheaper alternative is an arsenal of makeshift scraping tools (*inset*): dowels sawed off at an angle, an old screwdriver, a nutpick and a selection of stiff-bristled brushes.

Rinse the woodwork with the solution recommended by the manufacturer—most strippers can be rinsed with plain water or detergents, but some require a special neutralizer. Rub the rinse along the grain with coarse steel wool.

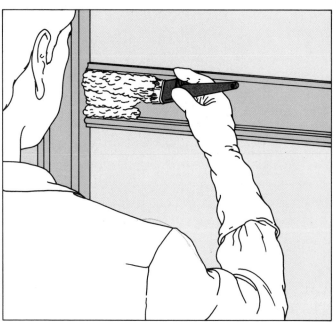

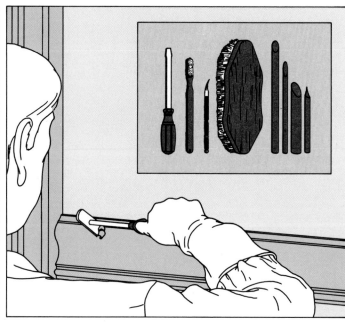

Special Tools for Taking Off Paint

Stripping with a heat gun. Set a heat gun—a device resembling a hair dryer, available through electrical-supply stores—at 700° and move it slowly back and forth, 2 to 4 inches away from the molding surface, until the paint begins to bubble up from the wood. If the paint does not bubble within a few seconds, raise the temperature, but always work evenly to avoid scorching the wood. Scrape the paint away with the same tools you would use with a chemical stripper.

Stripping with a heating iron. Hold the face of the heating iron on the surface of the wood just long enough for the old finish to begin bubbling. To keep from scorching the wood, frequently pick up the iron and scrape at the paint—when it comes free easily, remove the heating iron and finish scraping the patch.

Finishing the job with a sander. Use an orbital sander and medium-grit sandpaper to sand traces of finish off flat molding (*right*). Then sand by hand back and forth with fine sandpaper. Follow along the wood grain to remove any swirl marks. For rounded surfaces, use an electric drill fitted with a large, flexible-flap sanding wheel or a smaller, flapped sanding drum (*inset*); both are widely available at hardware stores. Do not use a wheel with wire flaps. For small, concave surfaces, glue a layer of felt around a small dowel, then hold sandpaper around it to form a sanding block (*inset*).

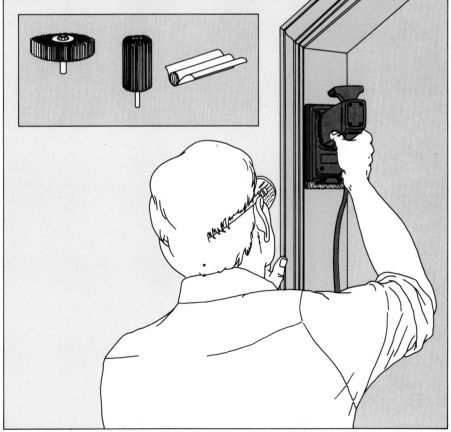

Freeing Fragile Woodwork for the Stripping Tank

1 **Loosening a brittle molding.** First carefully separate the paint joints between the trim and the wall, using a putty knife. Insert the blade of one putty knife between the wall and the piece of trim, then force in a second putty-knife blade directly beneath the first. Lightly hammer a thin cold chisel—or old screwdriver—between the two blades, loosening the woodwork slightly.

2 **Cutting the fastening nails.** Use a keyhole hacksaw to cut the nails holding the woodwork and gently pull the woodwork away from the wall with your hands. File down the nail stubs or pull them out through the back of the molding. Do not try to pound them out through the front—you may splinter the delicate face of the wood.

As you remove the trim, pencil a number on the back of each piece and enter that number on a sketch of the room. Later go back and scratch the numbers deeply into the end grain of each molding with a scriber or knife. Written marks will disappear in the stripping tank. To protect long moldings during transport, lash them to a 2-by-4 with cord or masking tape.

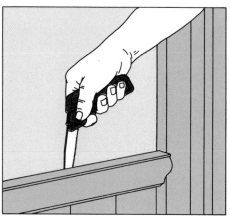

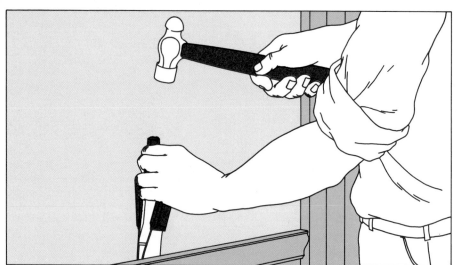

Filling a Gouge and Shaping the Patch

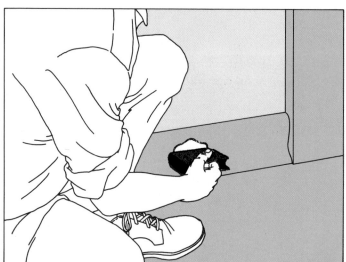

1 **Helping the filler adhere.** To roughen the surface of a shallow depression, gently tap a scattering of holes into the wood with a $\frac{1}{32}$-inch nail set. Fill the gouge with vinyl spackling if you are going to apply paint; use water putty if you plan to stain or varnish, wood putty for areas of heavy wear—door casings, window frames and the like. Force a thin layer of filler into the nail-set holes with a putty knife, then build upon this layer to the surface of the wood.

2 **Sculpting the patch to shape.** Shape the filler closely to the contours of the molding with the edge of a putty knife or with your fingers, but leave at least a slight bulge. After the patch is completely dry, sand it to shape with fine sandpaper. A sanding block formed by wrapping sandpaper around an old deck of playing cards, as shown above, will conform to the contours of the trim and will permit you to apply even pressure to the various irregular surfaces.

Carving a Molding to Match

When a section of wood trim is damaged beyond repair or is missing altogether, it must be replaced. Surprisingly many old moldings are still stocked by good lumberyards—especially in the shapes and sizes most common to the buildings in the locale. Sometimes, though, your trim will have to be duplicated from scratch.

For wide molding, it may be possible to reconstruct the contour by gluing and nailing together several simple stock pieces. Most molding contours, however complex, break down into a very limited number of classic molding shapes—and these shapes can be found in modern stock molding. Some old houses with very elaborate wood trim are already filled with such composites. More commonly, you will have to custom-mill pieces from molding lumber—generally white pine or poplar.

It is possible to cut many molding shapes with a router, or with the variously shaped blades that can be fitted on a multiplane. The most practical approach, however, is to use a table saw. You will need to fit the saw with a molding cutterhead—a special tool that mounts three identically contoured blades and fastens onto the saw arbor. Cutterhead blades come in some 50 different shapes; by using two or more blade shapes in separate passes of the saw, you can duplicate many complex contours precisely.

Select the proper blades by physically matching them to a sample piece of your molding. If this is not practical, trace the profile of your molding onto a cardboard template or pick up its profile with a contour gauge—a tool with a row of tiny pins that will silhouette whatever contour the gauge is pressed against. (Use such a tool carefully, as the pins tend to slip.) Some molding shapes will require that a cutting edge be custom-ground. If this is necessary, it may be more economical for you to take the whole project to a professional.

Cutting moldings on a table saw demands the utmost caution: Many of the tool's normal safety devices cannot be used with the molding cutter and the cutter blades themselves must be finely honed to make sufficiently precise cuts. Before starting the saw always double-check to make sure that the molding blades are securely fastened onto the cutterhead (below), and that the cutterhead itself is properly mounted on the saw arbor. Always use some hold-down device (page 40, Step 3) to secure the molding stock in line as it passes over the blades, and use a push stick to finish a cut. Stand to the side of the board being cut—never behind it.

1 Preparing the saw. With the table saw unplugged, remove the blade, blade guard, splitter and antikickback assembly. Slide a straight-edged planing blade into a slot of the molding cutterhead and secure it by tightly turning in its setscrew with a hex wrench. Attach the remaining blades and install the cutterhead on the saw arbor in the same way as you would a saw blade, including any special collars or reducer bushings called for in the cutterhead assembly directions. Drop the molding insert into the table surface to surround the cutterhead, then manually turn the cutterhead through one full revolution to check all parts for clearance.

2 **Notching an auxiliary fence.** Face the rip fence on both sides by screwing to it two straight-grained hardwood 1-by-3s to make an auxiliary fence. Lower the cutterhead below table level and move the auxiliary fence so it overhangs the top of the molding blade by ¼ inch. Start the saw and raise the cutterhead slowly about 1 inch to cut a semicircular notch in the fence. Turn off the saw and lower the blade. Move the fence closer, ¼ inch at a time, to widen the notch. Stop when the notch is three fourths of the way through the auxiliary fence. Move the rip fence to the other side of the cutting blades and notch the other section of the auxiliary fence.

3 **Making a hold-down.** Lay a piece of molding lumber against the rip fence, place a wood block atop the molding and clamp the block snugly to the side of the fence. This hold-down block will keep molding pressed firmly to the blades when the saw is running. To keep the molding aligned while it is being cut, clamp a second board to the table flush against the edge of the molding lumber. Reposition this second guide each time the rip fence is moved.

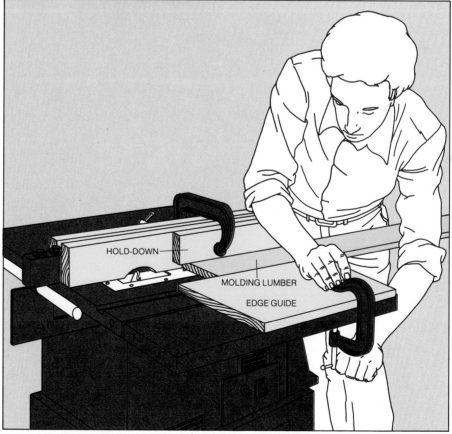

HOLD-DOWN

MOLDING LUMBER

EDGE GUIDE

4 **Using a set-up board.** Trace the contours of your molding onto a stiff piece of cardboard, then transfer the outline onto the end grain of a 6-foot length of molding lumber. Set the cutting depth and rip-fence position so that the cut will be slightly outside the traced line. Turn on the power, push the stock over the blade, check the results and adjust the blade depth and fence position until the cuts match the outline. Now run the set-up board all the way over the blades, using a push stick to finish the pass and taking care to stand to one side of the board being cut.

When changing the blade for subsequent cuts, similarly check the position with this same set-up board. The insets illustrate the sequence in which a fairly complicated contour can be cut in three passes over the saw.

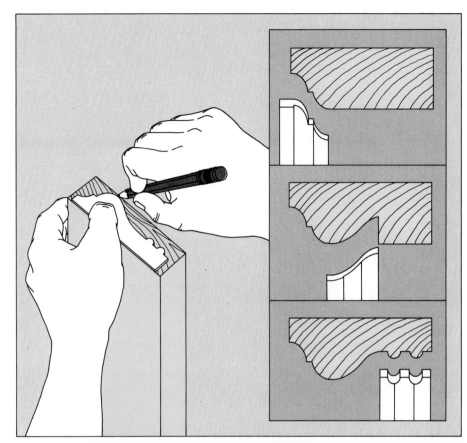

5 **Cutting the molding.** Use a push stick to feed the lumber through the saw. If the work begins to chatter, or vibrate, slow the rate of feed. If the chatter continues, lower the cutting depth and make the cut in two passes—marks left by chattering are difficult to sand smooth.

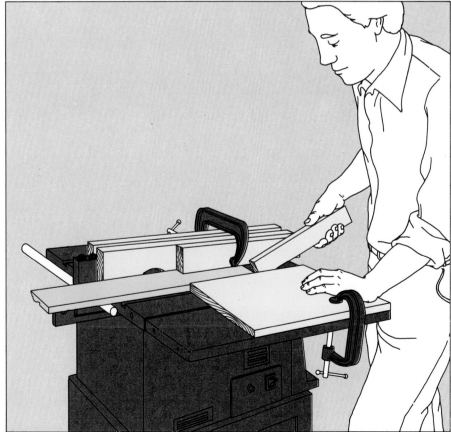

Plaster Repairs, from Nailholes to Grape Molds

Plaster is so durable that some has survived from classical times. But this ubiquitous building material, as common in old houses as odd-shaped corners, is also brittle, and it deteriorates if it is damp for a long time. Fortunately, small plaster blemishes—in walls, ceilings or decorative moldings—are easily repaired.

Wall and ceiling cracks can be quickly fixed with vinyl spackling compound or a fiberglass patch (pages 96-97). For chipped or cracked ornamental molding, use dabs of plaster applied with the spoonlike end of a pointing tool (page 44, top). Holes in plaster walls, if not more than 4 inches in diameter, are similarly simple to remedy: First stuff wadded newspaper into the hole, then moisten the edges with water and fill in the remaining depression with patching plaster or spackling compound applied in layers.

More serious damage, however, requires replacing large sections. For badly damaged walls and ceilings, the most convenient replacement method consists of nailing rectangular pieces of gypsum wallboard to the old lath, studs and joists, then smoothing the joints with wallboard joint cement. Old plaster is rarely of uniform thickness. In most cases it is necessary to insert thin strips of wood behind the new piece of wallboard to make it flush with the surrounding good plaster.

Major flaws in decorative plaster moldings are also repaired by the replacement of an entire section. Small molds of a good area, made with a water-based clay available in artists' supply stores, serve for one-time casting of small replacement segments—a few grape leaves, for example. You need not remove the original molding from the wall to make the mold. Larger sections—up to 5 feet long—are duplicated in plaster on a workbench.

The simplest molding to duplicate is called running molding, the type with smooth, continuous lines. Professionals once shaped it directly on the walls by pushing a metal template through a strip of wet plaster. They still use a template but the wet plaster is on a workbench and the hardened molding is installed in sections. Marble provides the best work surface, but an adequate alternative is plywood sealed with shellac, then lubri- cated with motor oil or a mixture of petroleum jelly and kerosene.

A more elaborate process, much like bronze casting, is used to duplicate moldings with intricate designs. For a model, first try to find an old discarded piece. If none exists, you must remove a good section from the wall, but practice this casting technique on some stock molding first—casting from a house molding involves some risk and you should be sure of your skill before endangering an irreplaceable piece.

Once the section is removed from the wall and placed on a workbench, it is covered with a thin layer of clay. Plaster is then poured over the clay to form a heavy shell 2 inches thick. After the plaster shell hardens, the clay is removed. When the shell is positioned back on the original, there is enough space between them to pour in a liquid cold-mix rubber molding material, an expensive liquid available at plastics-supply stores. After it sets, this rubber reproduces perfectly, in reverse, the design of the original in a thin, strong, flexible mold that can be used again and again.

No matter what the type of molding, mixing the plaster is a simple task. Sprinkle molding plaster into a bucket half-filled with cold water until the bucket is almost full. (Molding plaster contains no lime so it can be handled safely.) Beat the mixture for one to two minutes with a paint mixer attached to a power drill. The consistency of the plaster will vary—the warmer the workroom and the more stirring you do, the faster the plaster will harden. The mixture should be the consistency of thick oatmeal if you are going to use it to make shells, of honey if it will be poured into molds.

Once set, the moldings are cut to size with a wood saw and miter box. Construction adhesive, with additional support from flat-headed brass screws driven into joists or studs, holds each section in place. Joints and screw heads are then concealed with plaster.

Large Patches for Walls and Ceilings

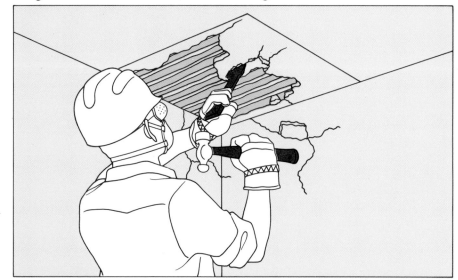

1 Removing the plaster. Use a chalk line to mark a rectangular area that extends just beyond the damaged area. The sides of the rectangle that run parallel with the joists should line up with joist centers; others should form right angles with these. Score the plaster along these lines with a utility knife; then, with a hammer and cold chisel, chip away the plaster, working from the damaged area to the scored lines. Remove rectangles of plaster from damaged walls the same way. Cut wallboard and wood strips to fit easily into the openings.

Caution: Remove only a small portion of plaster at a time—the blows can damage adjacent plaster. If cracks appear outside the chalk lines, patch them (pages 96-97), but if loose plaster starts to sag or fall outside the lines, remove it and patch the opening with wallboard. For safety, wear goggles and a respirator.

2 Attaching wood strips. Leaving the lath in place, edge each opening with wood strips fastened with small common nails driven partway into the joists, studs, lath and nailing strips. Use a scrap of wallboard to check how closely its surface matches the surface of the plaster, then drive thin shims between the strips and the lath until the wallboard is almost flush with the plaster. Finish driving the nails through the strips and saw off the protruding shims.

3 Installing the wallboard. Fit the piece of wallboard you have prepared for the ceiling into place and nail through the wallboard corners into the wood strips, lath and joists. Finish securing the wallboard to the joists with nails 6 inches apart. Install wallboard on the walls the same way.

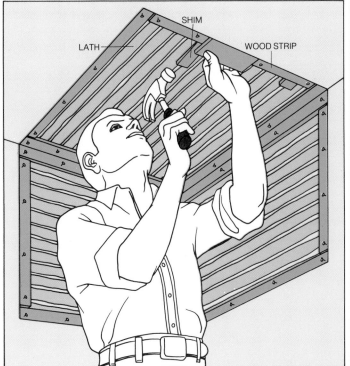

LATH   SHIM   WOOD STRIP

4 Taping the joints. Using a 6-inch-wide wallboard taping knife, spread a ⅛-inch-thick layer of joint cement over all the joints, embed perforated joint tape in the wet cement, and apply just enough wet cement over the tape to make the wallboard level with the plaster. Extend the top layer 2 inches beyond the edges of the lower one. Where surfaces meet to form a corner joint, apply the top coat on only one side of the joint.

Let the compound dry 24 hours. For straight joints, apply a final coat, feathering out the cement 6 inches on either side. For corner joints, apply an upper coat to the side skipped the previous day, wait another 24 hours and, if necessary to achieve a level surface, repeat with final coats on both sides—one side per day. When the cement is dry, sand with fine-grit sandpaper.

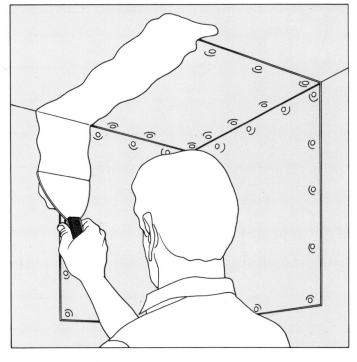

Sculpting an Ornamental Shape

Using a pointing tool. A special pointing tool, used by plasterers to round joints and fill cracks, can be used to press stiff plaster onto dampened, damaged molding a teaspoonful or so at a time. The tool has a differently shaped blade at the opposite end; it can be used to sculpt the design. Use a moist soft-bristled watercolor brush to smooth the plaster, to refine the design and to remove tool marks.

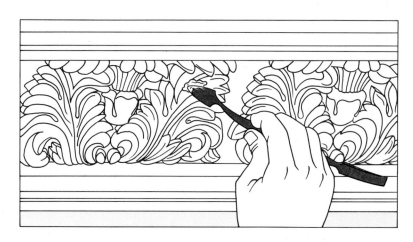

Molding with Clay

1 Making the mold. To ready the surface of undamaged molding for the clay that will transfer its design, dust a section of molding that duplicates the damaged one, brush on shellac and let it dry, then brush on a mixture of 3 parts kerosene and 1 part petroleum jelly. Press into place an inch-thick slab of clay, and over it spread a ¼-inch layer of thick plaster. Embed a piece of burlap and add a second coat of plaster. After 30 minutes, use a putty knife to pry carefully along the plaster backing, thus removing the clay-and-plaster mold from the molding.

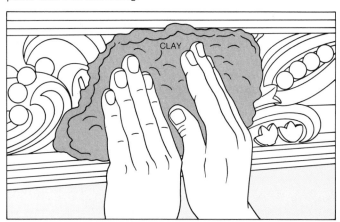

2 Pouring the cast. Spray a light mist of water on the clay and pour in a thin mixture of plaster. Jog the mold so any air bubbles will rise, then press cheesecloth on top. After about 10 minutes, pour on a second layer and form a flat back by pulling the edge of a ruler across the top. Let the cast harden about 30 minutes.

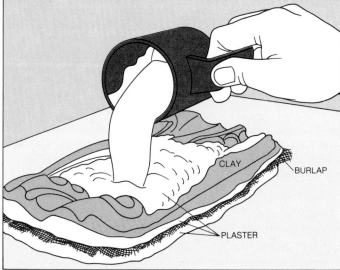

3 Fitting the cast. With a sharp wood chisel, cut away the damaged molding to form a depression slightly smaller and shallower than the cast; check the fit of the cast, then shave down its back and edges with a forming plane until the cast slips into the molding. Using a utility knife, score the back of the cast and the area into which it will fit; this will help the adhesive hold fast. To the back of the cast, apply ⅛ inch of construction adhesive, or more if it is needed to bring the cast out flush with the old molding. Set the cast in place and slide it back and forth to even the adhesive. Use a pointing tool and plaster to conceal the joints between the old and the new molding.

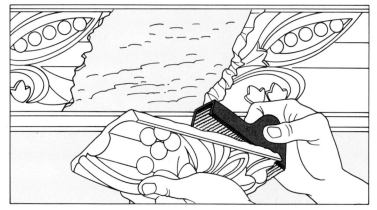

Shaping with a Jig

1 Tracing the profile. Drill a hole in the ceiling at the molding's front edge and, starting there, use a keyhole saw to cut through the molding from top to bottom *(right)*. Slide a piece of cardboard 1½ inches longer and wider than the molding into the kerf. With a sharp pencil, trace the molding profile on the cardboard *(far right)*.

Cut a sheet of .04-inch aluminum 1½ inches longer and wider than the cardboard. Tape the cardboard on top of the aluminum—aligning the corner of the cardboard that entered the plaster with a right angle of the aluminum sheet—and place them on a flat surface.

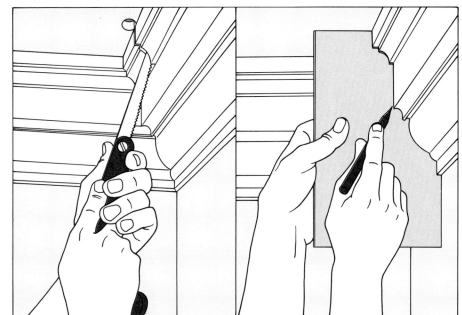

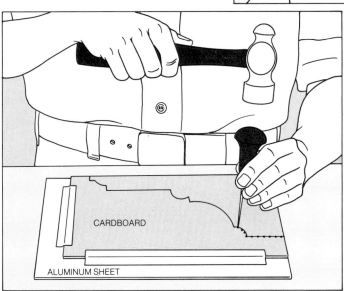

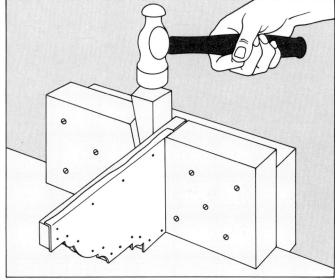

2 Making the template. Using an awl and a hammer, make pinpricks every ⅛ inch along the penciled profile line. Remove the cardboard and, with tin snips, roughly cut the profile marked on the aluminum. File the profile to the pinpricks and smooth with fine-grit sandpaper.

Place a scrap of 1-by-6, 1 inch longer than the aluminum, below the aluminum sheet, aligning it in the same position as the cardboard had been. Trace the aluminum profile on the 1-by-6, then duplicate this line ¼ inch inside the first. Cut along the second line with a saber saw; let the 1-by-6 extend 1½ inches past the aluminum's length. Set the aluminum atop the 1-by-6, projecting ¼ inch on the profile edge, and nail it with brads every ½ inch along the profile, every 2 inches along the other edges. If necessary, bend excess aluminum over the top edge of the 1-by-6.

3 Securing the template. Set the template in a jig made of 2-by-6s and lock it in place by driving a wedge between the template and jig. To make the jig, cut three pieces of 1-by-6: Make them 12, 6 and 5½ inches long. Cut a wedge 1 inch long at the top from the 6-inch piece. Screw the short pieces to the long piece—with outside ends of the short pieces flush with the ends of the long piece and their lower edges ¾ inch above the lower edge of the long piece.

Check that the template's top edge is square with the jig face, then tack a 1-by-2 diagonal brace from the jig end to the template end.

4 **Preparing the worktable.** With the jig snugly against the front edge of the workbench, have a helper hold a 1-by-12 upright against the far edge of the template and mark the 1-by-12's position. Repeat at 6-inch intervals down the length of the 1-by-12. Use these guide marks as you nail cleats to the bench along the back of the 1-by-12. Then add diagonal braces from the top edge of the 1-by-12 to the workbench surface beyond the 1-by-12.

Apply two coats of shellac to the work area of the 1-by-12 and the workbench, letting each coat dry, then brush a lubricant such as petroleum jelly mixed with kerosene on the board, bench, bench edge, template and jig.

5 **Making the run.** Pour a ½-inch layer of plaster on the workbench next to the 1-by-12, then push the template and jig along the front edge of the bench, checking to make sure the template's far edge remains snugly against the 1-by-12 during the run. After each run, add more plaster. Work quickly to stay ahead of the swelling of the setting plaster, but always take the time to clean plaster from the template with a putty knife before making the next run.

Complete the job by filling any missed areas with plaster and making a final run. Allow 20 minutes for hardening, then score the end edges of the molding with a wood chisel and pull the new molding away from the board.

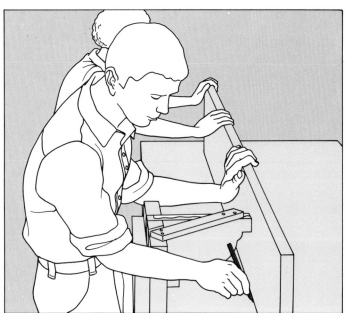

Casting Intricate Moldings

1 **Removing the old molding.** With a helper pushing against a good section of molding to keep it from falling, use a hammer and sharp wood chisel to score a line where the molding meets the wall and ceiling, to break the paint-and-plaster seal. At several places, slide a wide putty knife beneath the molding and gently pry the molding up. You should find joints in the molding every 5 feet. If you do not, the molding was made in place and you will have to remove a section by making two saw cuts (*page 45, Step 1*). Slip your fingers beneath the loosened molding and pull it from the ceiling and wall.

2 **Positioning the model.** Set the molding on a workbench so that its wall edge is against the table; support the molding at this angle with mounds of wet plaster at 1-foot intervals. Also use plaster mounds to support a 1-by-12 so that when it is laid flat atop the plaster, its top is flush with the inside edge of the molding that fitted against the ceiling. At each end of the molding, use plaster to prop squares of thin wood at the angle of the molding.

Seal the molding and the wood pieces with two coats of shellac. When this is dry, brush on the lubricant and cover the molding, including edges, with a sheet of flexible plastic that can be cut from a plastic garbage bag.

3 **Covering the molding.** Drape ¼-inch-thick clay slabs over the molding face and edges. See that the clay is smooth and does not lap over itself in a way that could create problems when you remove the plaster shell on top of it. Make ½-inch-thick clay strips, press them along the molding edges, and smooth any depressions. Then, for funnel holes, fashion 2-inch tapered clay mounds; just below the top edge of the clay, attach a mound at each end and one about every 7 inches between (*inset*). Lubricate the clay, the table and the 1-by-12.

Starting at the top, coat the clay with thin plaster. Add a second, ½-inch-thick layer, reinforce it with burlap and add a third plaster layer.

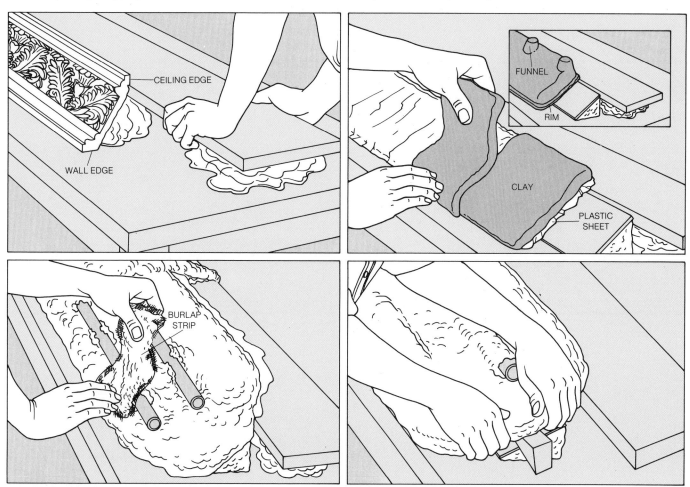

4 **Making the shell.** In order to reinforce the heavy shell, cut two pieces of ½-inch pipe the length of the molding. Set one along the top, one along the bottom of the wet plaster. Near each end, drape a 3-inch-wide, 1-foot-long plaster-soaked piece of burlap across both pipes, and then apply a fourth coat of plaster.

Allow the plaster to dry for about an hour. When the edges of the plaster begin separating from the workbench, mark the outline of the shell on the workbench and the 1-by-12.

5 **Removing the shell.** With a helper, use putty knives to pry up the plaster shell, put wedges under it, and then lift it off the clay. Set the shell on its back in another work area.

Remove the plastic and clay from the molding. Check the molding for chips and patch any that need fixing (*page 44, top*).

6 **Venting the shell.** Using a wood chisel, chip 2-inch-diameter holes in the tops of the funnel mounds. Then drill ¼-inch vent holes between every two funnel holes and also every 7 inches around the rim that is formed by the clay strips. File down any rough or high spots appearing within the shell and turn the shell over.

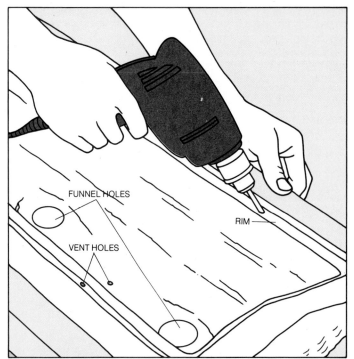

FUNNEL HOLES

RIM

VENT HOLES

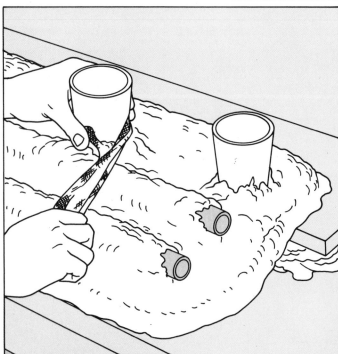

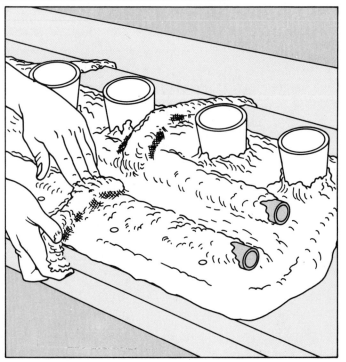

7 **Setting the funnels.** Cut off the bottoms of 12-ounce paper cups, set the cups atop the funnel holes, and seal them there with strips of plaster-soaked burlap 3 inches wide.

With a helper, stand the shell on end. Shellac the inside of the shell to seal it, then grease it liberally with petroleum jelly. Reposition the shell on top of the original molding, still on the bench; carefully align the edges with the marks that you made in Step 4, page 47.

8 **Securing the shell.** To hold the shell immobile, set two strips of plaster-soaked burlap between funnel holes, wrapping an end of one strip under the bench edge and an end of another over the back edge of the 1-by-12. Seal the shell edges to the bench and backing with plaster and put a piece of clay next to each vent. Then mix the liquid rubber, available at plastics stores, according to the manufacturer's instructions.

48

9 **Pouring the rubber.** Fill all cups with liquid rubber and have a helper plug the vent holes, one at a time, with clay as rubber oozes out. Keep pouring into the funnels until the rubber no longer sinks in them. Each cup should contain about 1 inch of rubber. Check the edges of the shell for leaks, then let the mold set overnight.

Chisel off the funnels and burlap ties, pry up the 1-by-12 and lift the plaster shell off the rubber.

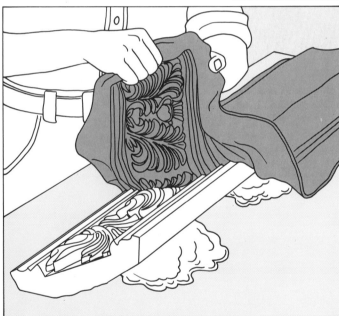

10 **Removing the mold.** Use a utility knife to cut off any excess rubber that protrudes from the vent and funnel holes; then lift an edge of the rubber and slowly peel the whole piece off the original molding. Replace the rubber in the shell and spray a mist of water on the rubber.

11 **Casting the new molding.** Pour plaster into the rubber form until the design is covered; jostle the shell to force the plaster into crevices and to force up any air bubbles. Add two more layers of plaster, reinforced in the middle with burlap. Then use a ruler to flatten the surface that will fit against the wall. Let the new plaster molding set about 30 minutes.

Turn the entire assembly over, lift the shell off the rubber and loosen the rubber edges from the new molding. Starting at one end, peel off the rubber form. Stand the new molding straight on end until installation, to keep it from warping.

The Enduring Beauty of Handsome Old Floors

Most old houses have wood floors of a kind difficult to duplicate today and well worth considerable effort in reconditioning. They may be of unusual woods such as beech or maple, or may be laid in parquetry patterns now costly to make. If the floors are of plain oak, the boards are probably long, unmarred by piecing, and beautifully grained. Even floors of inexpensive pine or fir—woods once common in simple farmhouses—become handsome antiques if carefully restored.

Because wood is a very durable flooring material, reconditioning may require no more than cosmetic work: sanding and refinishing. To remove coats of paint and expose the original wood grain, to erase a surface stain or burn, or to restore the polish of a badly scuffed floor, rent a drum sander (get one with a tilt-up lever for the drum) and a special edger for hard-to-get-at areas.

More often, repairs followed by refinishing will be needed; but the repairs may be quite simple. A squeaking floor—a minor but annoying ailment especially common in older houses—can have any of several causes. A subfloor may have pulled away from the joists, the finish floorboards themselves may be loose, or the bridging between joists may be insufficient or missing entirely. If a subfloor and the joists beneath a floor are accessible, repairs for all these ailments are easy. You can steady a loose subfloor by wedging shims between it and the joists, anchor loose flooring with screws driven up through the subfloor, or install prefab-

ricated steel bridging to stabilize joists.

If the ceiling under the floor is finished, the bridging area is relatively inaccessible—you must take the ceiling down to get at it. To eliminate squeaks caused by finish flooring, force powdered graphite, talcum powder, or glazier's points into the joints between the boards; if squeaks remain, drive and set finishing nails through pilot holes. If the problem is a loose subfloor, the remedy is simpler and surer: refasten the subfloor to its joists by driving nails down through predrilled pilot holes in the finish floor.

Other common defects in old flooring, somewhat more serious than squeaking, include sagging beneath cast-iron radiators, wide cracks between floorboards, and holes left by the removal of pipes—you often find them around radiators. These too are easily repaired, with 2-by-4 supports and post jacks (available from rental agencies), waterproof filling and plugs. Do not neglect such repairs or put them off: they correct genuine danger spots in the structure of a floor. Extensive sagging in a floor is a still more serious matter. It is a symptom not so much of faulty flooring as of weakened girders or joists below. The cure, shoring or jacking up joists and girders (pages 112-121), is a relatively heavy job, but a simple one.

While these simple techniques provide remedies for many flooring problems, one or two spots may require more drastic surgery. Some boards may be completely missing, others so badly warped or rotted that they must be pried out and

replaced. In parquet flooring (page 53), the job presents no particular difficulties. Another special case occurs in the many older houses that have strip flooring—interlocking tongue-and-groove boards fastened directly to the floor joists without any subfloor.

To replace floorboards in a house without subflooring, first determine the location and direction of the joists (generally indicated by the lines of end joints between boards), and plan to cut through the boards directly over a joist, so that you will have a nailing surface for the ends of the replacements. As you choose the sections of boards for removal, remember that end joints between boards must be staggered. And keep your patches as small as possible.

The unusual size and look of old boards give your floor its character—but the same features make it difficult to find suitable replacements. One way around the problem is to use replacement boards taken from inconspicuous places in the house—closet floors, for example, or the areas under rugs or furniture—and to replace these boards with new wood. Another is to forage among local wreckers and salvagers for old flooring; a third—the most expensive—is to custom-order duplicate flooring at a mill. Whatever method you choose, you will still have the problem of matching the stain for the new boards with that on the old. This final stage of a refinishing job can be tricky: always experiment on scrap pieces of flooring before staining a floor patch.

A Simple Brace for a Small Sag

1 **Locating the radiator from the basement.** Drill a small location hole through the floor alongside each radiator leg, then poke lengths of wire down through the holes so that later you will be able to find them from below.

2 **Installing supports.** Use the location holes as guides to position two 2-by-4 supports cut to fit between adjacent joists directly beneath the radiator legs. The supports will run along the length or width of the radiator, depending on the direction of the joists. Raise each support against the subfloor or floorboards with a post jack and have a helper upstairs check the floor as you raise the jacks; when the floor is level, face-nail through the joists to secure the supports.

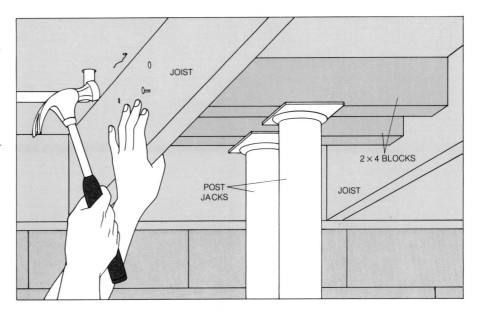

Quick Fixes for Gaps and Holes

Plugging holes left by radiator pipes. Wood plugs are the strongest fillers for holes, but in out-of-the-way areas, corks are the quickest and easiest fillers to use. Pound into the hole a greased cork slightly larger than the hole. Chisel off the protruding end and sandpaper the surface flush with the floor. The cork can be stained to match the surrounding floor fairly closely.

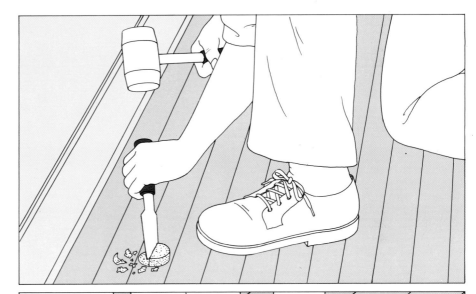

Filling cracks between boards. Fill small cracks with a paste made with 4 parts sanding dust (taken from an inconspicuous part of the floor) to 1 part penetrating sealer. For wide cracks use an old broad-blade putty knife to stuff lengths of felt weatherstripping into the space, filling each crack to a level ⅛ inch below the floor surface. If the weatherstripping shows, fill the last ⅛ inch with the paste used for small cracks. Some old floors, of course, have cracks so wide they cannot be filled; these are left open to preserve the floor's original character.

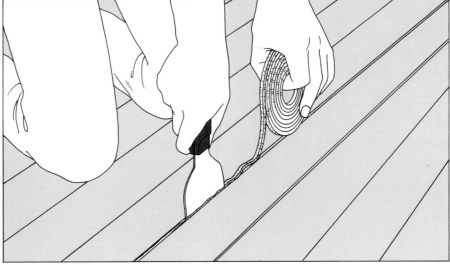

The Right Way to Sand a Floor

1 The first drum sanding. Wearing goggles and a respirator, start at a corner of the room, tilting the drum away from the floor before you turn the motor on; then, when the sander reaches full speed, lower the drum to the floor. On parquet or herringbone-pattern floors, use medium paper and move diagonally across the floor; on standard strip flooring, use coarse paper and move along the grain of the wood. Keep the sander in constant motion, always allowing it to pull you forward at a steady pace.

At the far wall, tilt the drum up, swing the cord out of the way, and pull the sander back over the area you just sanded. When you return to the starting point, lift the drum and move the sander left or right to overlap the previous pass by 2 or 3 inches. Continue with forward and backward passes, occasionally turning off the sander to empty the dust bag. When you have sanded the entire room, run the sander along the unsanded strip against the wall.

2 The first edge sanding. Use the edger, loaded with the appropriate paper for your floor, to sand the areas missed by the drum sander; the rotating disk of an edge sander can be moved in any direction on the wood.

Repeat the drum and edge sandings, using medium paper for a second sanding and fine paper for a third. On herringbone-pattern or parquet floors, do the second sanding on the opposite diagonal to the first and do the final sanding along the length of the room (*inset, top*). On standard strip floors move the drum sander along the grain for each sanding (*inset, bottom*).

When you have completed all three of the sandings, remove the old finish in tight spots—under radiators and in corners, for instance—working along the grain with a sharp paint scraper. Then sand these areas by hand.

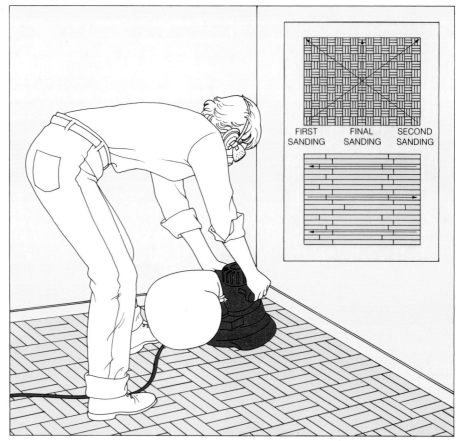

FIRST SANDING   FINAL SANDING   SECOND SANDING

Durable Patches
for Damaged Parquet

1 Removing the damaged piece. If the parquet does not have tongue-and-groove joints, insert the blade of an old 3-inch putty knife into a joint next to the damaged piece and gently pry it out. If you have trouble loosening the piece, move the knife along the joints, prying at different spots. When the piece has been removed, pull any nails that have worked through the wood and remain embedded in the subfloor.

On a parquet floor with tongue-and-groove joints, use a chisel to split the damaged piece down the middle, then pry out each half.

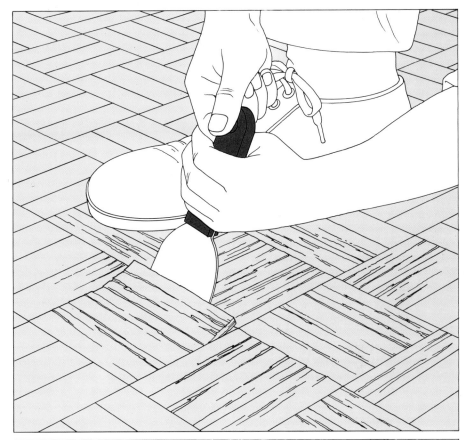

2 Inserting a new piece. Fit the new piece into place and tap it down with a mallet. If the other pieces of the floor are face-nailed, drill pilot holes, matching the nailing pattern of the rest of the floor. Nail the new pieces down with four-penny resin-coated nails. If the floor is tongue-and-groove, blind-nail through the tongue as you would for strip flooring (*page 55, Step 5*).

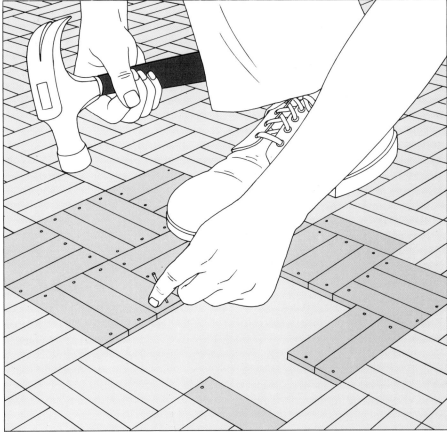

Fitting Replacements for Tongue-and-groove Boards

1 Freeing the floorboards. If there is no subfloor under the flooring, free each damaged section of a floorboard by the following techniques. If the end of the damaged section lies within the span of the floorboard, as shown here, chisel straight down over the center of the nearest joist, with the bevel of the chisel facing the damaged area. About 1 inch closer to the damaged area, drive the chisel, bevel up, toward the vertical cut at a 30° angle. Repeat until you have cut through the board. To free a section of a floorboard from the joist at the end of the floorboard, omit the vertical cut; instead, chisel at an angle to cut away the end of the board. Free both ends of all sections to be removed.

Use the same general techniques to free sections of flooring over a subfloor, except that when you cut a board in the middle of its span, the vertical cut need not be directly over a joist.

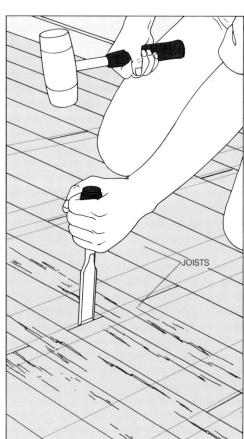

JOISTS

2 Removing the boards. To avoid damage to tongues and grooves of undamaged boards, split each board to be removed into three strips. Starting at the middle of the damaged section, chisel two parallel incisions along each board to be removed. Rock the blade in the incisions to split the board.

Insert a small pry bar into a split at the center of the damaged area and carefully pry out first the middle strip, then the groove side, and finally the tongue side of the board. Working from the center outward, pry up the remaining boards in the same fashion, then remove or set any exposed nails.

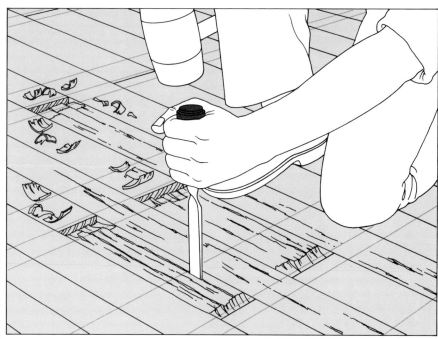

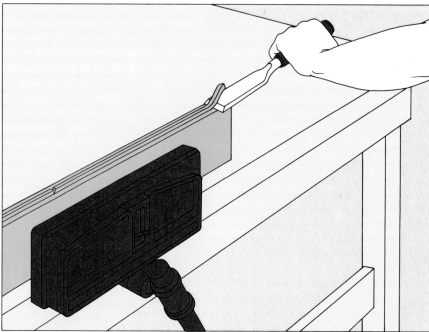

3 Cutting the tongue from a board. For a room with a subfloor, this step is unnecessary; go to Step 4. In a room without a subfloor, new sections of flooring must end over joists, the joints in adjacent rows must be staggered and part of each new floorboard is generally fitted between two boards already in place. To prepare a board for fitting, secure it tongue side up in a vise and chisel off the tongue along the part that will fit between two boards. Make a vertical cut across the tongue to mark the section to be removed, then tap the chisel, bevel up, against the end of the tongue to split it off only up to this cut.

4 Inserting the new boards. In a room without a subfloor (*below, left*), tilt the groove of the new board downward alongside the tongue of the preceding course, fit the groove of a scrap of floorboard over an untrimmed section of the tongue and tap the scrap gently with a mallet to snug the board into place.

In a room with a subfloor (*below, right*), fit a new board between two existing boards by the following method. Lay a piece—cut at least 3 inches longer than the part between the boards—flat on the subfloor, work the tips of its tongue and groove into place, and then use a scrap hammering block to tap the piece in.

In any room, insert boards that do not fit between two boards already in place by the following method. Use a piece of scrap wood fitted over the tongue of the new piece as a hammering block while you drive the board into place, positioning the grooved side of the new board over the tongue of the preceding course.

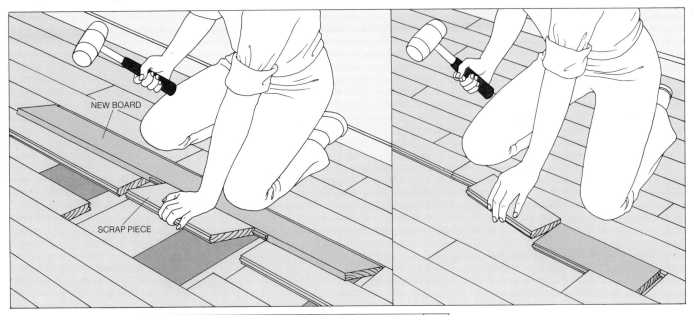

NEW BOARD

SCRAP PIECE

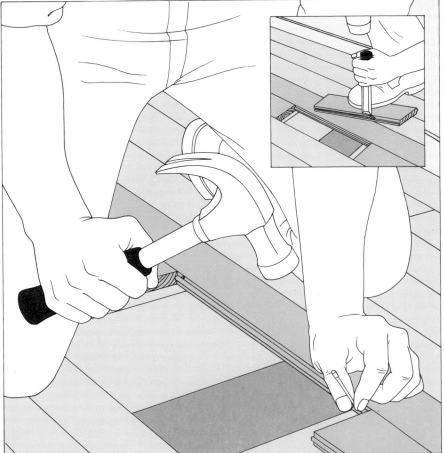

5 Blind-nailing a board in place. Drive and set eightpenny finishing nails at a 45° angle through the top corner of the tongue of the new board into each joist below the board. Wherever blind-nailing is impossible—as at the ends of the board shown here—drill pilot holes and drive eightpenny finishing nails down through the board face, ½ inch in from its edges. Set the face nails and cover them with wood filler tinted to match the color of the floorboard.

To fit the last board in place—whether or not there is a subfloor—use the chisel to remove the lower lip of the groove along its entire length (*inset*), tap the board into place tongue first, and face-nail it to every joist.

Getting Balky Doors and Windows to Work Right

Doors and windows are among the balkiest parts of an old house, and for good reason: they are exposed to the ravages of the weather, their hardware wears out from constant use and their operation is easily impaired by warping and sagging. To make matters even more difficult, the very construction of your old doors and windows may call for special tricks of repair or adjustment.

Most older houses have double-hung windows and all too often one of the sashes—generally the top one—is frozen shut. Typically, the sash is glued shut by layers of paint and can be freed by the method shown below. Occasionally, however, a sash is nailed shut. To locate the nails remove the stops and, for a top sash, also remove the lower sash and parting strip. Pull the frozen sash partway out of its frame. Only then can you cut or pull the nails behind the sash.

Built-up paint can also cause a sash to stick, rather than freeze, in its frame—and a reluctant sash is almost as irritating as a frozen one. To solve the problem, scrape and sand away the paint; you should not, ordinarily, plane the sash or move its stop. Unsealed wood swells during a humid summer and a sash scraped

or planed at that season is likely to rattle during the winter; the best time to treat the sash is during dry autumn weather.

Occasionally sashes jam because moisture has loosened the glued mortise-and-tenon joints at the corners of the sash frame. Pin the loosened joint with a wooden dowel, then paint the wood and renew putty around the window panes.

In some windows, broken sash cords can be replaced by what is now the conventional method, in which the sash weight is temporarily removed through an access plate in the side jamb. In many older window frames, however, there is no plate; the side casing must be removed before you can get at the weights. While the sash is out, consider replacing the unbroken cord as well, rather than waiting for it to break; if your windows have metal pulleys with wide grooves, you can replace both cords with indestructible metal sash chains.

As an old house settles, doors and doorframes become particularly vulnerable to racking and sticking. Once again, conventional remedies are available. On a rattling door you can move the stop molding or cover the stop with weather stripping; on a door with loose hinges,

you can use longer hinge screws or glue wooden dowels (matchsticks will do) into screw holes. Some unconventional but ingenious solutions can be tried: You can shim an old-fashioned two-knuckle hinge with washers, perhaps, or use toothpaste to determine the correct position of the strike plate.

Pocket doors, the handsome, paneled sliding ones that disappear into the walls of many Victorian houses, have special problems. There are two types—doors that roll along a metal floor track, and doors that hang from an overhead track. The hardware is no longer manufactured for either type. Moreover, diagnosis of a problem is complicated by a bewildering variety of construction methods, and the problem itself is often beyond reach, deep inside the pocket. If the methods shown on pages 61-63 fail, the only solution is to remove a section of plaster from the wall to get at the root of the trouble.

Panel doors—whether pocket type or hinged—are vulnerable to another ailment: joinery loosened by age, moisture or paint-stripping chemicals. But the remedy is simple: squaring the doors and reglueing them, then reinforcing the loosest joints with heavy-duty dowels.

Loosening Up a Sticky Window

Freeing frozen sashes. Outside the house, try to free the top sash by tapping the blade of a 6-inch putty knife into the joint between the sash and the blind stop, working along the sides and top of the sash; if necessary, repeat the procedure between the bottom sash and the parting strip. Inside the house, tap the blade between the top sash and the parting strip and between the bottom sash and the interior stop.

If the sashes remain frozen, go outside the house, wedge a general-purpose prying bar between the sill and the stile at one corner of the lower sash, and pry the sash up, using a wooden block for leverage. To get at the top sash with the bar, pry the top parting strip out of its channel with a wood chisel; you may first have to remove the lower sash (*opposite, Step 1*) and the side parting strips. Inside the house, wedge the utility bar between the head jamb and the top sash and pry the sash down.

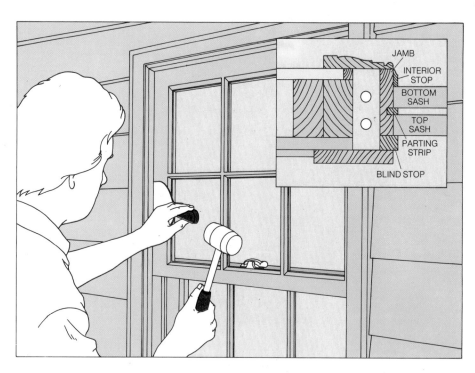

Easing a tight channel. Using a wood chisel with the bevel edge against the wood, pare away paint and dirt from the sash channels in the jamb and from the edges of the stop and parting strip. Sand the channels until they are smooth, using a wooden sanding block slightly narrower than the channel; then lubricate the channels with a block of household paraffin.

Fixing a Broken Sash Cord

1 Removing the lower sash. Remove the side stop (page 38, Steps 1 and 2) next to the broken cord, then raise the sash slightly and angle its side free of the jamb. Rest the sash on the window stool (the interior sill) and pull the cord end out of its slot in the sash with long-nose pliers.

If your window has interlocking weather stripping—the type that fits into a groove in the sash—remove it at the same time that you pull out the sash. Remove the side stop and have a helper raise the sash to the top of the frame. Use carpenter's nippers to remove the nails that fasten the weather-stripping track, then angle it out of the window frame along with the sash.

On a window without an access plate (a rectangular wooden insert in the side jamb that provides access to the sash weights), remove the casing that conceals the sash weights and set the sash back in place between the jambs. On a window with an access plate (inset), untie the cord on the other side of the sash, make a large knot in the end of the cord to keep it from slipping over the pulley and set the sash aside. Remove the screws or nails that hold the access plate and pry it out with a chisel; if you must, remove the parting strip to get at the plate.

2 **Threading the new cord.** For a window with no access plate, knot the new cord to the counterweight, at a point about 3 inches from one end of the cord. Feed the other end over the pulley and pull it down to the corner of the sash.

For a window with an access plate, tie a piece of string to a bent nail and feed the string over the pulley until the nail appears at the access hole; then tie the other end of the string to the sash cord, use the string to pull the cord down, and tie the cord to the weight. Set the sash on the window sill and retie the unbroken cord.

3 **Adjusting the cord.** Pull the cord down until the counterweight reaches the pulley, then lower the weight about 2 inches. Thread the cord through its slot in the edge of the sash, knot it and trim off the loose end. Set the sash in its channel, raise it to the top of the frame and check the height of the counterweight: it should be visible in the exposed front of the window framing or through the access hole, suspended about 2 inches from the bottom of its compartment. Replace the casing or access plate, then fasten the stop with threepenny finishing nails; longer nails would interfere with the sash weight.

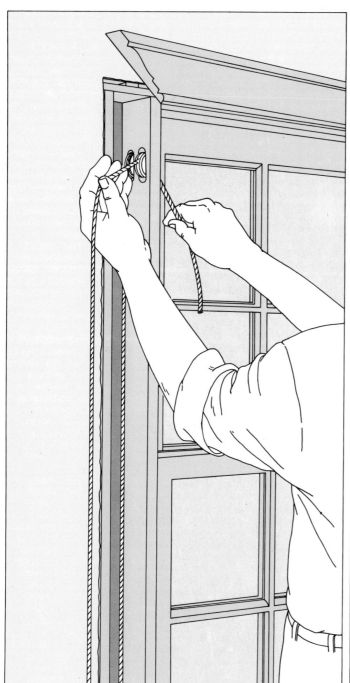

Pinning the Corners of a Weak-jointed Sash

1 Drilling a dowel hole. Place the sash or door on a workbench, with its outside face upward, and clean out the loose joint with a wire brush. Apply glue liberally to both sides of the tenon and force the joint tightly closed with a bar clamp. Then place a drill guide on the stile, ½ inch from the joint and opposite the center of the rail, and drill a 5/16-inch hole about ⅛ inch shallower than the thickness of the sash or door.

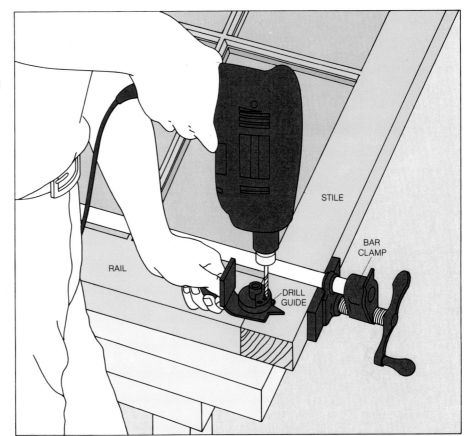

2 Pinning the tenon. Cut a fluted wooden dowel— a type available at hardware stores, with pre-cut grooves for glue—to the approximate length of the hole; coat it with white glue and tap it into the hole with a mallet. After the glue sets, trim the end of the dowel flush with the face of the sash or door and sand the surface smooth.

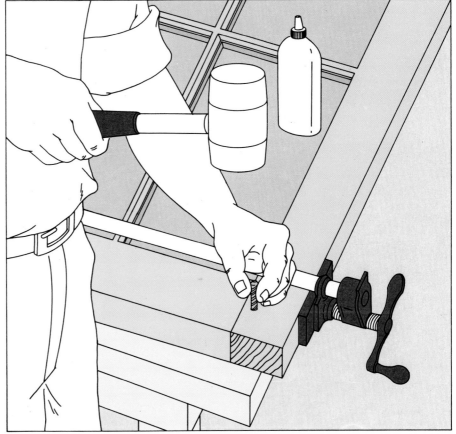

Making a Door Fit Its Jamb

A door that scrapes the floor. Each hinge on an old-fashioned door ordinarily has two knuckles: a lower knuckle with a built-in pin, and an upper knuckle that slides onto the pin. Lift such a door off the pins of the lower knuckles and slide washers onto the pins. Experiment with washers of different thicknesses until the door no longer scrapes; the thickness of each set of washers should not exceed ⅛ inch.

If washers will not stop the scraping or if your door has hinges with interlocking knuckles and removable pins *(inset)*, loosen the screws fastening the lower hinge to the jamb and wedge the bottom of the door up slightly. Cut cardboard shims with slots for the screws; slide them behind the hinge leaf, experimenting to find the correct thickness, then tighten the screws.

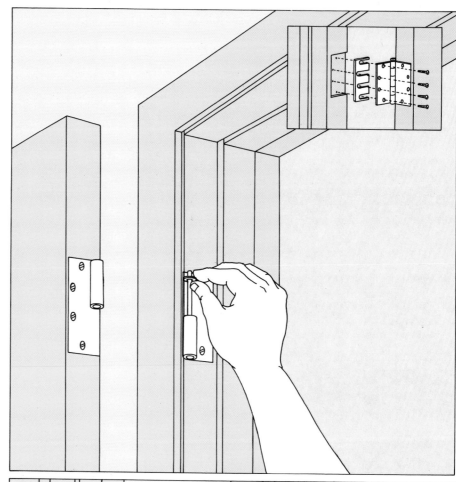

A door that will not latch. Remove the strike plate, squeeze toothpaste into the mortise and the bolthole behind it and smooth the toothpaste flat with a putty knife *(right)*. With the doorknob turned to hold the latch bolt open, close the door; release the knob of the closed door, then turn it again to retract the bolt and open the door. If the imprint of the bolt in the toothpaste is more than ¼ inch off center *(far right)*, align the strike plate with the imprint and mark around it for a new mortise and bolthole. Scrape away the toothpaste and enlarge the mortise and bolthole with a wood chisel. Replace the strike plate and fill the exposed portions of the old mortise with wood filler.

If the imprint is less than ¼ inch off, clamp the strike plate in a vise and enlarge the strike opening with a file; do not enlarge the mortise.

A door that binds against the jamb. If the door sticks at the top or along a small part of the side jamb, tap a wedge beneath it to hold it open and use a block plane to pare away the edge that binds, making a $1/16$-inch gap between the jamb and the closed door.

If an entire side binds on the strike side or hinge side, remove the door and unscrew the hinges. Mark a line $1/8$ inch from the hinge edge and have a helper hold the door on edge while you plane down to the line with a jack plane. Test the fit of the door and mark any points that require additional planing; when the door fits correctly, deepen the hinge mortises, reattach the hinges and replace the door.

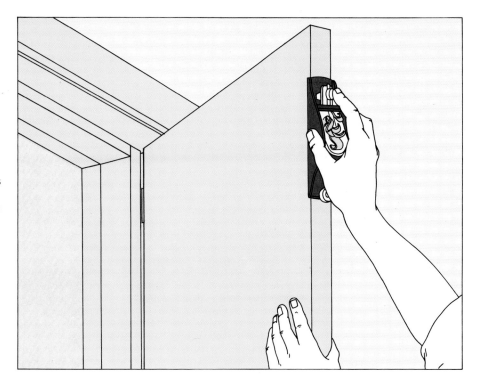

Freeing a Sticky Pocket Door

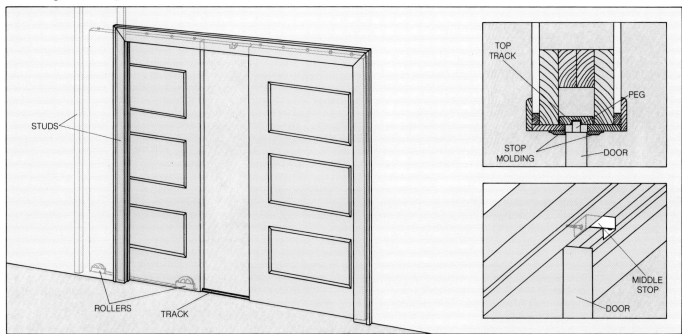

Diagnosing the problems. These typical pocket doors ride on grooved metal wheels along a raised metal track. Inside the wall, the doors fit into pockets framed by pairs of narrow wood studs. Each door's top fits between stop moldings; in some, wooden pegs fit in a grooved track to hold the door in line (*inset, top*). Double pocket doors have a metal stop screwed to the edges of the jamb (*inset, bottom*) to keep doors from sliding beyond the middle of the opening.

In older houses, the studs in the pockets sometimes warp and bind the door; to detect such studs, you must first remove the door from its pocket. Unscrew the center stop and slide the door to the opposite side of the doorway. Probe inside a pocket with a piece of scrap wood as wide as the door and notice where the scrap binds. Studs at the edge of the opening can be planed easily; to reach studs deep within a pocket, remove part of the plaster wall covering.

The rollers at the bottom of the door may be broken; matching rollers are no longer manufactured, but you may find replacements in secondhand shops or improvise new sets from large window pulleys. Bits of plaster often pile up in the pockets; this debris can be swept or vacuumed out. Within the opening, a floor track may be dented or crushed; you can bend the track back into shape with pliers after removing the doors and the nails that fasten the track.

Retrieving a jammed door. Screw metal eyes into the edge of the door, about 4 feet above the floor and a foot apart. Run a loop of heavy wire between them and use the wire as a handle to drag the door out of its pocket.

Removing a door from its frame. Unscrew the center stop of a double door and slide the door to the center of the opening. Pry off one of the stop moldings from the top jamb and, while you bend the grooved track above the door upward with a scrap of lumber, have two helpers lift the door off its bottom track and gradually slide the bottom of the door sideways until the top of the door is free. For a single door, you must remove the casing, jamb and stop at one end.

Shaving a warped stud. Remove the door or, in a double door, remove the center stop and slide the door to the far side of the opening; then remove the casing, jamb and stop that cover the warped stud. Wearing goggles and working from the middle of the stud toward the top and bottom, shave away about ⅛ inch of wood with an electric drill fitted with a drum-rasp attachment; move the drill slowly and apply a light, steady pressure. If studs at the back of the pocket are warped, break through the plaster to get at them, then follow the same procedure.

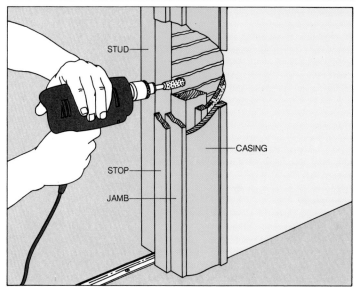

STUD

CASING

STOP

JAMB

Improvised replacements for rollers. Cut a block of wood as thick as the deep mortise in the bottom of the door, wide enough to fit snugly between two large window pulleys set within this mortise, and long enough to reach the top of the deep mortise and line up with the shallow faceplate mortises at each side. Cover the block with glue, tap it into the center of the deep mortise and fasten it with fourpenny finishing nails. After the glue sets, fasten window pulleys to the door bottom on each side of the block, using No. 6 wood screws 1½ inches long (*inset*).

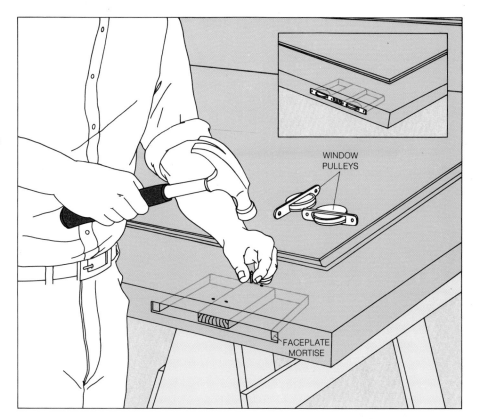

WINDOW PULLEYS

FACEPLATE MORTISE

Adjusting Doors that Hang from Above

Fixing doors that scrape the floor. As an old house settles, doors that hang from trolley glides and roll along an overhead metal track begin to scrape along the floor. To adjust such a door, move it to the center of the opening and tap shims beneath it to lift it ¼ inch from the floor, then tighten the adjustment screws on the rollers above each end of the door. If the adjustment screws are not visible at the ends, or if the door has a third roller between the outer ones, remove one of the top casings that conceal the metal track, so you can get at the screws. You must also remove the casing before you can adjust a door that has a hexagonal adjustment bolt rather than screws.

To remove newer, hollow-core doors, lift door and trolley off the overhead track; such a door usually has a hexagonal adjustment bolt (*inset*).

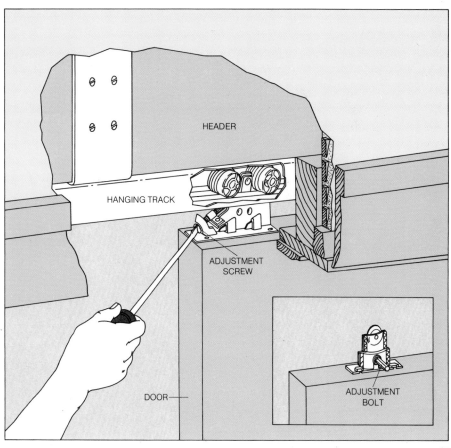

HEADER

HANGING TRACK

ADJUSTMENT SCREW

DOOR

ADJUSTMENT BOLT

Doweling a Door to Correct a Sag

Squaring the door. To recondition a panel door that has sagged because of loose framing joints, first prepare a work surface by nailing or screwing two 2-by-4s along two of its edges at a right angle. Dismount the door and lay it on the work surface. Carefully spread open the loosest joints and apply glue to the inner surfaces; some hardware stores sell syringe-like glue applicators that are especially suited for such tasks. Be careful not to spill glue onto any joint between a panel and the surrounding wood—the panels must be able to move freely within the slots provided for them or they will crack as the door swells and shrinks in different seasons. Before the glue dries, square the door by forcing it into the right angle formed by the 2-by-4s. A bar clamp (below) will be helpful if the joints are stiff. Once the door is squared, release this clamp; use it and two others to clamp the door across the width. Wipe away any excess glue with a moist cloth.

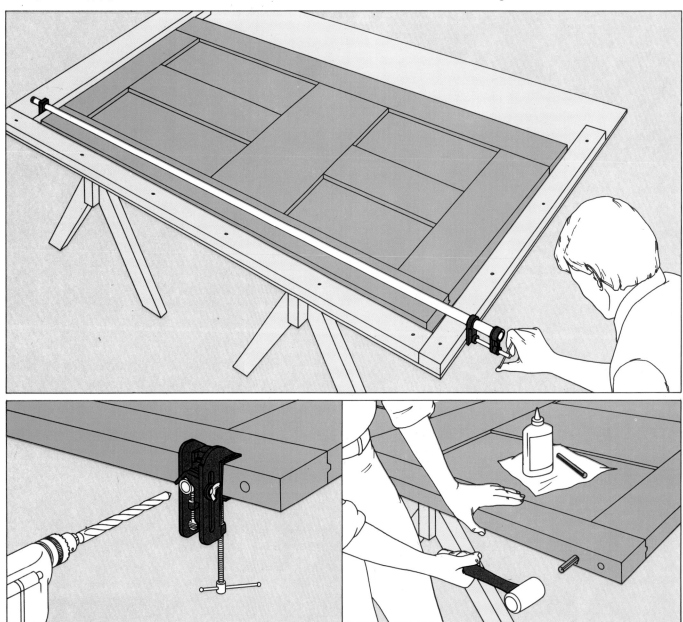

Reinforcing a weakened joint. After 24 hours, remove the clamps and position the door so that you can work on its edges. At the weakest joints—usually the ones at the bottom—drill two holes ½ inch in diameter as far as your drill bit will go into the two joined members. A guide such as the dowel jig shown above will help you to drill straight.

Cut fluted wooden dowels (page 59, Step 2) to the length of the holes. The precut grooves in the dowels will provide an outlet for the glue; without an outlet, pressure put on the glue when the dowel is inserted into the hole may lead to splitting the surrounding wood. Apply glue to both the insides of the holes and the dowels, and then tap the dowels into place.

Clamp the door again if the joint opens, and allow the glue to dry.

If you are going to paint the door, sand the dowels flush. If you are going to stain it, make the dowels ¾ inch shorter and fill the ends of the holes with plugs—available at hardware stores —whose wood and grain match the door edge's.

Hand-hammered Nails and Quartersawed Hemlocks

Authentic restoration requires of the doers a rare degree of patience, skill, historical knowledge, taste and devotion. It also helps a great deal if the house they are restoring has nobility of character to sustain them when the going is toughest.

Such a fortunate pairing of people and place occurred in 1975 when Fred and May Hill, a young New York couple looking for a modest weekend retreat, came upon a dilapidated 18th Century farmhouse in the hills of northwestern Connecticut. The price was right, the setting delightful, but the house was, in their words, "a charming ruin." Not fully aware of what lay ahead, they bought it. The saga of their labors and the gradual transformation of that old farmhouse stand as both a caution and an inspiration to anyone who is embarking on an authentic historic restoration.

At first, the Hills recall, their plan was to renovate, fix up and make the best of some modernizations that their predecessors had visited upon the house. But the more they poked about, the more they became aware that they had taken on not just any old house, but a public trust, the oldest house in their community and an outstanding example of the classic New England salt-box design. They felt they had no choice but to restore the place to its original condition, circa 1740. To their astonishment, it was not long before they discovered that "the doing had become one of the most meaningful things in our life. It became our hobby as well as a deep personal education for each of us, something we shared intimately."

The Hills mapped a plan to take the house apart and put it back together in stages. That way, no matter how long it took or how disruptive any one project might be, they would always have some place to get in out of the cold. The salt-box's most pressing weakness was its lack of a convenient kitchen. Since this was one area in which the owners were willing to take modern liberties, they decided to add a new wing and install the kitchen there. A rotting 19th Century shed on the back of the house was torn down to make space, and framing,

with 18th Century barn timbers bought nearby, was erected in its place.

In the Hills' effort to ensure that the new wing was integrated architecturally with the outside of the old portion, the choice of clapboard was critical. Old clapboard, unlike the modern variety, was quartersawed from logs, producing a distinctive grain. The Hills found a mill producing small quantities of quartersawed hemlock, but traces of the modern rotary saw blade compromised the effect, so the clapboards all had to be sanded before being put into place. Hand-hammered iron nails, costing 11 cents each, were used to fasten them.

In the main section of the salt-box, the old walls and roof first had to be made weathertight. Windows, clapboards and shingles were removed and replaced in painstaking fashion. "In the process," Fred Hill remembers with satisfaction, "we got to know the house intimately, to feel it down to its bones. The framing, which is really what an old house is all about, was 90 per cent sound. Having withstood two centuries of wind and rain and snow without damage, it is as strong today as when it was first built, if not stronger."

Locating some of the materials for the inside of the house proved a slow process. "We waited six months to find boards wide enough to replace those missing from the old pine paneling in the keeping room, for example, and we regularly went hunting for early hinges and latches and the like to make piecemeal replacements." Furniture, lighting fixtures and fireplace tools of the period were also gathered gradually.

Asked what rewards they get from living in a house that looks and feels so removed from our modern, fast-paced, efficient lives, Fred Hill answers without hesitation, "A house like this is a lot of fantasy. When we are here we feel a sense of communion with the past.

"We know who lived here, generation by generation. We know a good deal about how they spent their days and nights and how they passed the seasons. We feel part of a long line of families who lived good lives here, and to an extent we adopt their patterns without being too self-conscious about it. Beyond that, we feel a sense of responsibility fulfilled. We are fortunate to be in a position to save this house. We live in it, we enjoy it, we don't think of it as a museum. But we believe that the house has an existence and a value that transcends our period of tenancy, and we are proud to be its caretakers."

3

Making Do with Aged Utilities

The moment when the new owners of an old house are handed the keys is one of mingled joy and trepidation. Delight over the prospect of fine hardwood floors is tempered by concern about a dusty old fuse box. Anticipation of soft morning light through leaded glass in the pantry mixes with doubts about clanking pipes in the kitchen. Worries about the fitness of old utility systems can be a major concern: Outdated systems are expensive to replace, and life in the house during such a repair can range from awkward to impossible.

A good house inspection will have laid these fears partially to rest—the wiring is reasonably safe, the plumbing fairly sound, the fireplace and heating system old but serviceable—but doubts linger on. Household utility systems do have a limited life span. Yours will someday have to be replaced. In the meantime there are steps you can take to keep the old systems functioning.

Plumbing and wiring have undergone a number of changes since your old house was built, but the changes have largely been new developments in materials rather than fundamentally innovative ideas in design. The standardization of pipe sizes and layouts greatly simplifies plumbing repairs and makes it easy to find replacement parts. Where they are allowed by local building codes, plastic pipes and flexible copper tubing now make small replacement jobs simple; the development of a vast selection of adapter fittings allows you to repair any type of old piping material with almost any type of new material.

Similarly, innovations that have gained acceptance in the craft of household wiring have largely been in the range of materials that electricians have at their disposal. The concepts that went into your old-fashioned wiring will not often be hopelessly out of date. Old armored cable or conduit wiring may be practically in mint condition. And though it is usually too much to hope that the earlier knob-and-tube wiring will be suitable for long-continued use, even it can be kept safe for a time with vigilance and methodical repair.

Great strides have been made in the development of new heating systems. Modern systems are plainly cleaner, more effective and more convenient than their older counterparts. But replacing an old system is so expensive that it could be many years before the increased energy efficiency pays for itself. With the rising costs of energy, it is not unheard-of these days for an old-house buyer to clean up and repair even an old coal-burning furnace and then relearn the arts of kindling a coal fire and shaking down ashes from a furnace grate. Short of this, you can often improve the performance of an old heating unit substantially by making simple repairs or catching up on neglected maintenance.

Keeping Fireplaces Safe, Clean and Efficient

Fireplaces are among the most esthetically intriguing parts of an old house and they can be a practical asset as well: properly maintained and well fueled, they can reduce energy costs by allowing a lower thermostat setting for the central heating system. Unfortunately, many old fireplaces are not safe—about 30,000 house fires are caused each year by flame and heat from faulty flues and chimneys.

Before using an old fireplace for the first time, make sure that its crucial parts are still in safe condition. This applies especially to the flue liner—a duct, normally of terra cotta, that lines the chimney. If your chimney was built without one, or if the liner is in poor condition, you must install a new one—in a major renovation involving tearing away and rebuilding much of the chimney. Unless you have considerable masonry skill, this is a job for a professional.

If the flue liner is in good shape, you still must make sure it is clean; if it is not, it can cause a chimney fire. Such a blaze, burning with blast-furnace intensity, can spew flame and debris out of the fireplace and chimney top. Chimney fires occur most often when soot and creosote—a tarlike deposit—build up on flue walls and suddenly ignite. You can probably knock off these residues by lowering and raising a gravel-filled bag in the chimney. Very thick build-ups may need professional cleaning brushes.

Other parts of the fireplace that can deteriorate—the exterior chimney masonry, the firebox and the smoke chamber—most often do so because of the effects of either rain water or heat. If the chimney cap, the mortar pyramid atop the chimney, has cracked, it can let water in between the flue liner and the chimney. It should be patched or rebuilt and, for safety, be fitted with a steel-mesh screen to keep warmth-seeking animals out and large cinders in.

If enough rain water enters the chimney to puddle in the fireplace, a hood is needed for the chimney. This hood will also shield the chimney top from occasional downdrafts that can waft annoying puffs of smoke into the room below. If, however, your fireplace smokes chronically, you must improve the draft by reducing the size of the fireplace opening.

You can either lay firebrick on the floor of the firebox or install a glass screen to reduce the size of the opening.

A special problem in many old houses is the fireplace that has been covered over. You might be able to return such a fireplace to operation by simply uncovering it and restoring the hearth, but it is more likely that you will have to do extensive rebuilding to make it safe.

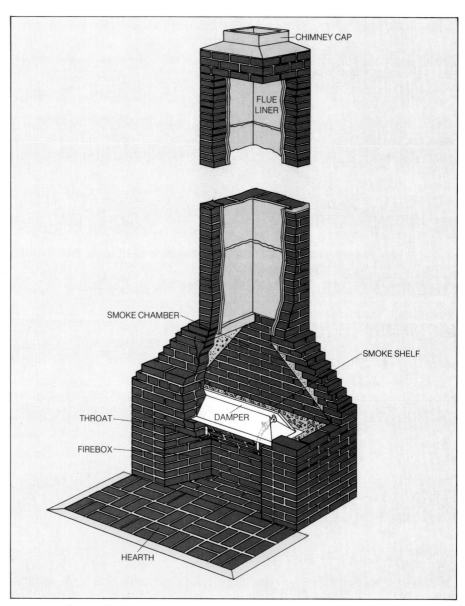

Inspecting a flue and fireplace. Working from the roof, lower a trouble light into the flue and examine the flue liner for large cracks or missing chunks of mortar, and for missing mortar in the joints between sections of the liner. If soot and creosote obscure the surface of the liner, remove enough of these deposits to allow inspection (*right*). Check the top of the chimney to see that the chimney cap is solid and uncracked. Caution: On a roof of more than moderate slope, always work from a ladder that is equipped with a roof hook hung on the ridge.

Inside the house, check the joint between the firebox floor and the hearth. Loose or crumbling mortar can be repaired with adhesive fireclay. See that the damper works and that the smoke shelf is free of debris. Examine the smoke chamber, the throat and the bottom of the flue liner; repoint (*page 123*) any bad joints.

Conducting a smoke test. See that the flue liner and smoke chamber are clean. Staple fireproof fiberglass insulation batts or a wet blanket to a plywood big enough to cover the fireplace opening. Prop several sections of newspaper on the smoke shelf above the damper and light them. When the fire is going well, close the damper to a 1-inch opening. Cover the front of the fireplace and have a helper on the roof place a wet towel over the chimney top. Check the length of the flue for smoke leaks, starting in the attic. Where the flue passes behind finished walls, look for leaks under baseboards or around frames of doors and windows. Have your helper check the chimney outdoors.

Once the test is done, uncover the chimney top and let the smoke clear for at least 15 minutes before uncovering the fireplace opening. Open the damper and clear off the smoke shelf.

Repairing the Chimney Top

Renewing the chimney cap. If the cap has deteriorated badly, don safety goggles and chip it off with a ball-peen hammer and a cold chisel. Clear away the debris and dust, then wet the area and trowel on mortar to form a sloping cap that extends from the edge of the brick to about halfway up the side of the top flue liner. Keep the mortar damp for four days for proper curing.

If the mortar cap is mostly solid but has crumbled in a few places, remove any loose portions, fill the gaps and cover the cap with new mortar. If the cap has only a crack or two, cover them with a fiberglass patch (*page 96*).

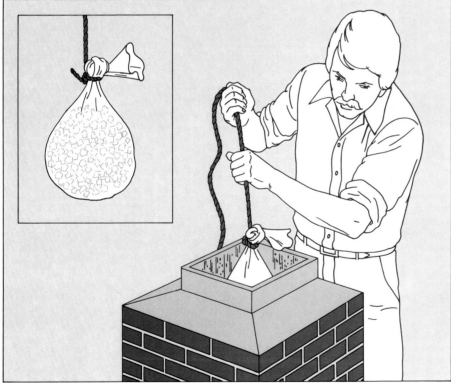

Cleaning the flue. Knot the neck of a small canvas or burlap bag filled with about 3 pounds of gravel, sand or chain; tie a ½-inch rope to it underneath the knot (*inset*). Open the damper and tape two layers of flexible plastic over the fireplace opening. From the roof, lower the bag slowly down the flue. Run it up and down a few times against each face. Wait an hour for the soot to settle, then unseal the opening and gently remove the debris with a rented industrial-type vacuum cleaner (soot can ruin a household vacuum) or a dustpan and whisk broom. Finally, clear the smoke shelf, sweeping debris into a paper sack held at the fireplace throat.

Making a screen of hardware cloth. Mark the in-side dimensions of the flue on the center of a 1-yard-square piece of ½-inch screen mesh, called hardware cloth. Extend the lines of the square to the edges of the cloth and cut away the corners with tin snips. Fold the mesh along the edges of the square to form a screen box that is open on one side. Insert the open end of the box into the flue so that the top is 6 inches above the top of the tile liner (*inset*), thus keeping animals out and hot cinders in.

Adding a chimney hood. After removing the chimney cap (*page 69, lower right*), lay bricks at each corner of the chimney to a height 6 inches above the top of the flue (*below, left*). Then make a new mortar cap around the bricks. Allow the mortar to set overnight.

Mix a handful of brick chips into a small amount of mortar and trowel the mixture onto the top of the supports (the chips will keep the heavy hood from squeezing out the wet mortar). Set the hood—a flat slab of rock or concrete cut slightly larger than the chimney by a masonry-supply company—onto the supports (*below, right*). Keep the masonry damp for four days.

Installing a Glass Screen

While a fireplace screen with glass doors can be beautiful, it has practical advantages as well: it can serve as a damper for a fireplace that has none; it can reduce the opening, to increase draft, and it can cut down the volume of warmed room air being sucked up the chimney.

The screen generally consists of two main parts—a frame that is held over the front of the fireplace with mounting brackets, and a set of glass doors that fit into grooves on the frame (they can be easily removed for cleaning). A screen may also include metal-mesh curtains to keep sparks in when the glass doors are open. Choose a unit with a frame large enough to overlap the side and top edges of your opening, but small enough to clear any decorative moldings. The best screens have fiberglass insulation packed around the inside of the frame to seal the gap between the screen and the front of the fireplace opening. Damper controls at the bottom, and on some screens at the top as well, allow flexibility in controlling the draft, which controls the rate at which the fire burns.

1 **Marking the bracket positions.** Attach the mounting-bracket and lintel-clamp assemblies loosely to the back of the screen frame (inset). Place the frame over the fireplace opening and adjust the clamps to fit the lintel. Turn the setscrew of each clamp until the tip touches the lintel or masonry inside the fireplace opening, then tap the setscrew with a hammer to mark the position of the tip. Set the frame aside.

SETSCREW
BRACKET SCREW
LINTEL CLAMP
MOUNTING BRACKET
FRAME NUT
FRAME

2 **Fastening the clamps.** Drill dimples—holes less than ¼ inch deep—into the lintel or masonry inside the fireplace at the points you marked in Step 1, to prevent the tips of the setscrews from slipping. Reposition the frame into the opening and tighten the setscrews, bracket screws and frame nuts. If your unit has additional brackets to support the bottom, drill holes for lead anchors at the bracket locations and screw the lower brackets to the hearth. Mount the metal-mesh curtain, if supplied, then insert the doors.

For a fireplace without a lintel, or for a screen frame that has brackets but not lintel clamps, drill holes for lead anchors into the fireplace masonry at the bracket positions and secure the brackets with screws. Some screens, commonly inexpensive ones, have simple thumbscrews instead of brackets; drill dimples at the thumbscrew locations, for a firmer installation.

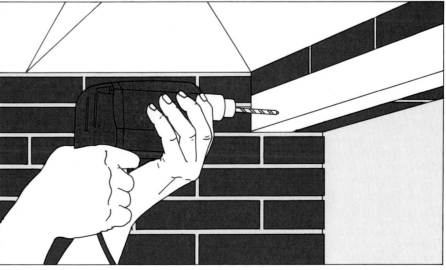

Coaxing More Heat from Radiators and Registers

Before the Civil War most homes were heated by fireplaces or stoves, and you can get by with such basic devices, even in cold winters, if you are prepared for a basic life style; quilts and long johns become essential. Most old homes, though, have central heat. Even so, the system may be one no longer common.

Until the 1930s, when electricity was increasingly used in homes, the modern schemes of blower-powered forced air and pumped hot water were rare. The old systems relied on convection to carry heat up through a home. Hot-water systems simply heated water and depended on its natural tendency to rise for circulation of warmth to radiators. Old hot-air systems were really little more than centralized stoves; a large firebox in the basement heated air that then rose through huge ducts, a separate duct for each room, creating such a bewildering complexity of arms running off in many directions that these furnaces earned the nickname octopus.

Some old homes need new heating systems: If you want to have central air conditioning or if the old heating system is hopelessly incapable of maintaining comfort, replacement may be the proper choice. But you can coax a surprising amount of additional heat from even the oldest of systems by catching up on any regular maintenance and repairs that were neglected over the years.

In a hot-air system, make sure that the dampers behind the registers are open; you may want to replace old-fashioned registers with modern adjustable deflector grilles that aim the heat toward a room's coldest parts. In steam systems, check to see that radiators are shimmed to tilt slightly toward the inlet pipe; if the valve of a steam or hot-water radiator leaks, the stem should be repacked or the valve replaced.

If your renovation plan calls for moving or removing radiators, you can replace them with baseboard convectors, long, finned pipes that mount unobtrusively along baseboards. The pipeworking techniques involved in installing them are discussed in the plumbing section of this book (pages 76-81).

If after making minor repairs or additions—and making sure that your furnace is clean and properly adjusted—you still have a cold room, the problem is solved most easily with a self-contained electric baseboard heating unit. Some can simply be plugged in, others must be connected directly to a power-supply cable in a junction box. The latter installation is preferable unless your heating season is short or the room is little used.

If the heating lack extends beyond one room, you can coax more heat from an old system by boosting hot-air circulation with an auxiliary blower, or hot-water flow with a circulating pump. The blower, wired with a thermostat and connected into a nearby junction box, will go on when the air in a duct begins to warm. After the burner shuts off, the fan will stop so it does not blow unheated air through the house. A circulating pump in a convection hot-water system can be wired to an aquastat—a thermostat for water—to turn it on and off as needed. Be sure the power is off before you begin electrical work (safety tips, page 83).

Tuning or Replacing a Troublesome Radiator

Packing a valve stem. After draining the system and twisting off the valve handle and packing nut, scrape out any old packing and wrap two or three turns of graphite-impregnated packing cord clockwise around the stem. Push the cord down the stem, replace the packing nut and tighten it just enough to stop the hissing when the system is refilled and turned on.

If you have leaks around other screw-together parts of the valve, try tightening them. If necessary, replace the valve: Using the plumbing techniques shown on pages 76-81, loosen the union between the valve and the radiator. Grasp the body of the valve with a pipe wrench and twist it off the threaded riser. When screwing the new valve into place, coat all threads with pipe-joint tape or compound.

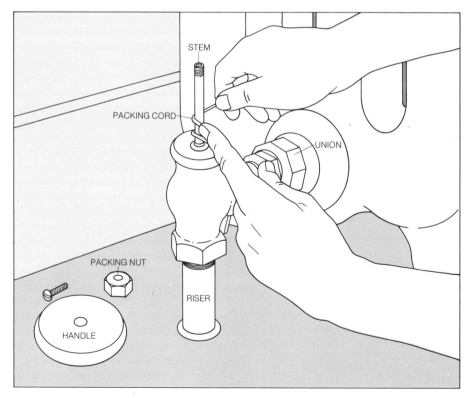

Installing a baseboard convector. After removing the old radiator, its risers and the baseboard behind it, screw the housing of the new unit, with allowance for carpet height, to the studs and fit the heating element into the brackets. Make the holes for the risers to the new unit and run flexible copper connectors from the riser connections to the elbow and to the valve on the convector. Install the cover and the end pieces, and reattach the wooden baseboard to the wall at each side of the unit.

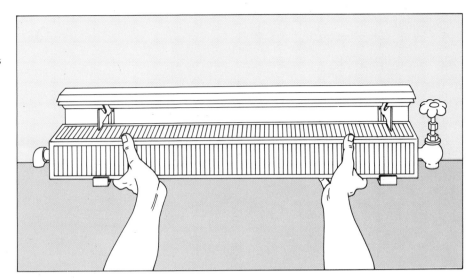

Adding a Hot-water Circulating Pump

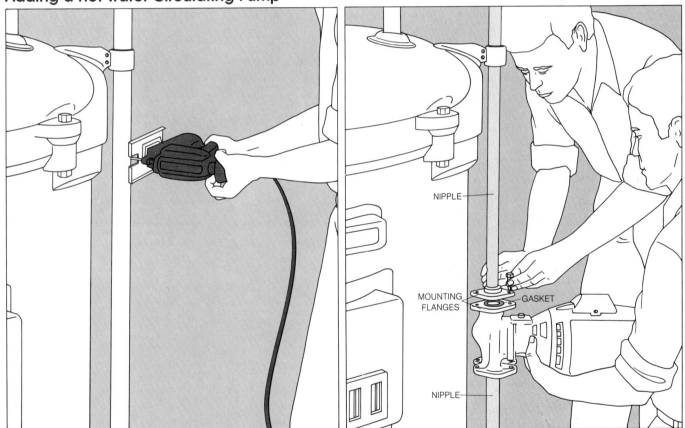

1 **Breaking into the return pipe.** Drain the system, then remove the vertical section of the return pipe that leads to the bottom of the boiler. Though professionals shatter the cast-iron elbow above the pipe with a hammer, it is safer to cut the pipe with a saber saw. Caution: Wear goggles. Unscrew the pipe sections and elbows, then screw on new elbows and also—if you must step down to a smaller size pipe to accommodate the pump—reducer bushings.

2 **Mounting the circulator.** Screw pipe nipples, threaded at both ends, in place of the old vertical pipe, leaving enough space between their ends to fit the pump, then attach the mounting flanges that come with the circulator. While a helper holds the circulator, place gaskets into its flanges and bolt these flanges to the mounting flanges with the bolts and nuts supplied with the pump. Rotate the motor—its mounting is adjustable—so that its oiling sleeves are upright.

3 **Wiring the motor.** Attach the straps of an aquastat around the supply pipe leading from the upper part of the boiler. Turn off the power supply to the nearest junction box—commonly there is one mounted right on the furnace—and run plastic-sheathed cable to it from both the aquastat and the circulator motor.

Connect the circulator and aquastat as you would a light fixture and switch (*inset*). At the circulator, connect the black and white wires of the cable to the matching wires of the pump motor and attach the cable ground wire to the circulator grounding screw. Attach the black and white wires of the aquastat cable to the aquastat terminals, recoding the white wire black at both ends with a dab of paint or a turn of electrician's tape. Connect the ground wire to the chassis of the aquastat.

In the junction box connect the ground wires together, join all white wires, join the black wire of the circulator to the white-recoded-black wire from the aquastat and join the black wire from the aquastat to the black wire of the power supply.

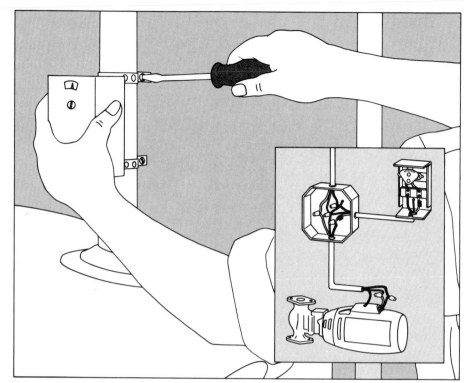

Giving Airflow a Boost

1 **Cutting the opening.** Drill a starter hole in a vertical duct, or in the top or bottom of a horizontal or angled duct, then complete the cut for the blower with a saber saw. The blower instructions will note the proper size for the opening; be sure to locate it so that the blower motor shaft will be horizontal, even if the duct slants.

2 **Mounting the blower.** Hold the unit in place, turned to blow air toward the registers, and mark through the flange screw holes. Drill pilot holes at the marks and fasten the blower in place. Bend the flanges to match the curve of the duct to keep warm air from leaking out, then attach the blower with sheet-metal screws.

3 **Fitting the thermostat.** Make a 1-by-1½-inch hole in the duct, for the thermostat probe, and secure the thermostat to the duct with sheet-metal screws. With the power shut off, run plastic-sheathed cable from a nearby junction box to the thermostat and the blower motor. As indicated in the inset, connect the black and white wires of the cable to the leads of the motor and connect the ground conductor to the green wire or grounding terminal. At the thermostat, connect the black and white wires to their terminals; fasten the ground conductor to the thermostat chassis with a sheet-metal screw. Recode the white wire black at both ends. At the junction box join all the ground wires together, join the white wires of the box to the white wire of the motor cable and join the black motor wire to the white-recoded-black wire of the thermostat. Join the black wire of the thermostat to the black wires of the junction box.

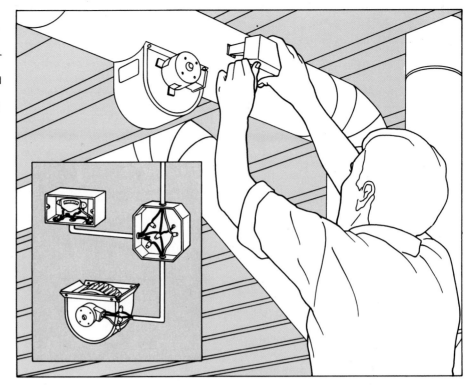

Electric Baseboard Heat

Installing the heater. Remove the baseboard and screw the heater to the wall studs; allow for carpet height. Run a plastic-sheathed cable from the service panel, or from a junction box containing a little-used circuit, to the heater. Connect the wires *(inset)* as follows: Join the black and white wires of the heater to the corresponding cable wires; join the ground wire of the cable to the grounding screw of the heater. At the junction box, wire black to black, white to white and ground to ground. You may want an electrician to make the connections at a service panel if you are not sure you can do the job safely.

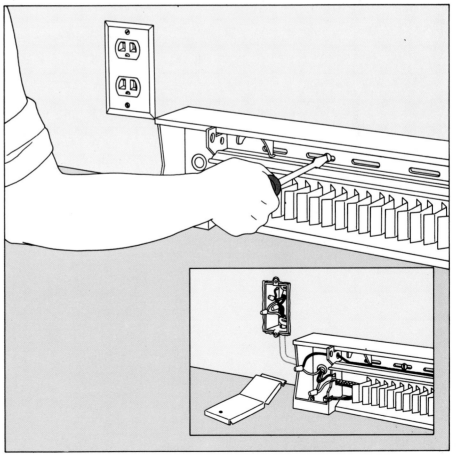

Renovating the Plumbing, a Little at a Time

Plumbing in many old houses is either obsolete or well on its way to becoming so. But the wholesale replacement of pipes is a big job that may mean tearing into interior—and sometimes exterior—walls. Unless your plans call for a major renovation of the house, you can extend the useful life of the plumbing you have for some time by patching it and renovating it piece by piece.

The most visible parts of a plumbing system—the tubs, sinks, lavatories and toilets—long outlast the pipes to which they are attached. The working parts of these fixtures—faucets, drain levers, toilet valves and the like—have remained basically the same over the years. In most cases modern parts can be used to repair old equipment.

A far more serious problem in old plumbing systems is the deterioration of pipes. The galvanized-steel supply pipes that were used in the majority of old homes may last 40 years at most before rust and corrosion rupture or clog them. Cast iron—the most common material for old drainpipes—has proved more durable. But it too can rust over the years. Steel piping eventually must be replaced, but the first leaks can be patched for the time being with the semipermanent patches that are shown below and at right: pipe clamps for leaks in straight runs and fiberglass bandages for leaks around joints and fittings.

Leaks around the joints of cast-iron drainpipes should be recaulked with lead. Though this job calls for working with molten metal, the straightforward configuration of the joints makes it a rather simple task. Old cast-iron piping is connected with lead-caulked bell-and-spigot joints. Each pipe section is made with a bell-shaped hub at one end and a plain spigot at the other.

To join pipe sections, the spigot of one piece is inserted into the hub of the next, the joint is packed with oakum—an oil-impregnated, ropelike fiber—and the space over the oakum is filled with molten lead. The lead is then caulked—that is, pounded into the joint—so that it will form a tight seal. Small leaks in these joints sometimes can be repaired by simply tamping down and reshaping the soft lead with a hammer and chisel or by

packing the joint with lead wool, a shredded lead product similar to steel wool.

If these simple measures are not sufficient to stop the leak, the leaking joint must be recaulked from scratch. You will need to rent a plumber's furnace, a cast-iron pot, an iron ladle, and yarning and caulking irons—offset, chisel-like tools that are used to pack down the oakum and lead. If you have to recaulk a joint in a horizontal pipe, you also will need an asbestos joint runner to direct the molten lead, since you cannot pour it directly into the hub. The plumber's furnace looks somewhat like a picnic stove but is constructed of heavier materials that will stand up to the higher temperature it produces. Some are fueled by gasoline, others by propane or acetylene. Ask the renting agency to provide you with complete instructions for operating the model that you select.

Wear long sleeves, gloves and safety goggles when you pour hot lead, and make sure the joint is completely dry be-

fore you begin. Any moisture in the hub will turn into steam when heated and will send molten lead splattering out of the joint. If the pipe seems at all damp, dry it by heating the outside with a propane torch. Stand behind the joint when pouring the lead and fill the cavity with one continuous pour.

Lead pipe is found in some very old houses. Since it is soft, repairing its leaks is difficult. Tightly clamped pipe sleeves will crush lead pipe, but minor leaks can be successfully repaired by using a fiberglass bandage (opposite).

Because chips of old paint with a high lead content are widely known to be very toxic, the buyer of an old house with lead water-supply pipes may be concerned. However, the risk in drinking water from lead pipes is almost nonexistent, since lead is insoluble in water. The Basic Plumbing Code of the Building Officials and Code Administrators International specifically approves the use of lead pipes for water distribution.

Simple Patches for Small Leaks

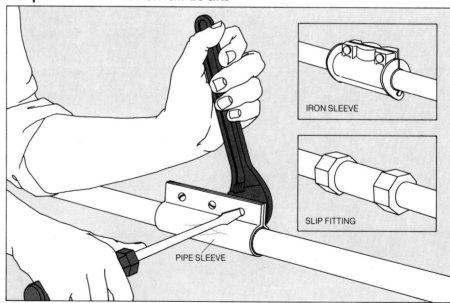

IRON SLEEVE

SLIP FITTING

PIPE SLEEVE

Using a pipe sleeve. To patch a minor leak, bend a rubber-lined metal pipe sleeve around a copper or plastic pipe, then tighten the nuts and bolts that hold it shut. A heavier iron sleeve, installed the same way, is designed for cast iron or steel. A slip fitting can be used as a coupling for a broken pipe or for a leaking pipe that is almost rusted through (page 81, bottom).

Bandaging with fiberglass. To apply a fiber-glass pipe patch, mix about ¼ cup of epoxy mastic and butter it on the pipe several inches on either side of the damaged section, as well as over the damage, with a wooden spatula. Wrap a strip of fiberglass cloth around the pipe, embedding it in the mastic. After the mastic has hardened, spread a second layer over the cloth.

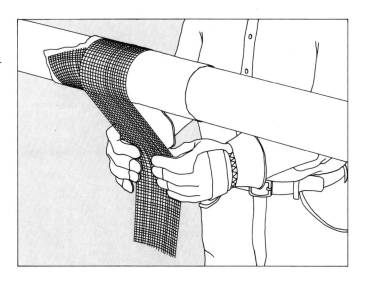

Recaulking a Joint in Cast-iron Pipe

1 Packing the oakum. Pry the old lead and oakum from around the leaking joint with a thin chisel or an old screwdriver. If it does not come out easily, heat the joint with a propane torch to soften the lead. Repack the hub with strands of oakum, ramming it down tightly with a hammer and an offset yarning iron designed for this purpose, leaving at least an inch of space at the top. See that no strands of oakum reach into this space.

Light the plumber's furnace and melt about 1 pound of lead for every inch of pipe diameter.

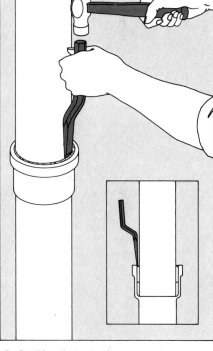

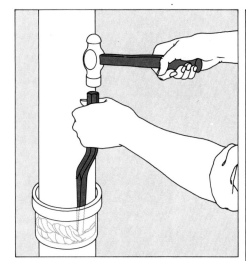

2 Pouring the lead. Heat the ladle in the flame, then use the ladle to push aside any dross or scum that has accumulated on top of the molten lead and dip out a ladleful. Pour the lead carefully over the oakum until it reaches the rim and curves slightly at the top. If the first ladleful does not fill the space, add more lead immediately. If you are pouring lead into a horizontal or pitched joint (*inset*), clamp an asbestos joint runner snugly around the pipe and push it tightly against the hub in order to channel the lead into the hub. Keep the clamped ends on top; pour the lead between these ends. Wait until the lead has hardened before removing the runner.

3 Caulking the lead. After the lead has cooled for at least 30 seconds, position the tip of an inside caulking iron, its beveled edge facing outward, against the spigot, and hammer the lead firmly into the joint with a ball-peen hammer. Drive the lead down about ⅛ inch to lock it into the joint.

To compress the joint, hold an outside caulking iron (*inset*) between the inside of the hub and the lead and tap it with a hammer until the top of the lead bulges slightly. (A caulking iron resembles a yarning iron, but is shorter and is beveled.)

Replacing Lengths of Worn-out Piping

If so much of the pipe in your house has deteriorated that simple repairs are impractical, you will have to cut out the bad sections and replace them with new. Luckily, the first pipes to deteriorate—the horizontal sections—are the easiest to reach. The vertical pipes, which run up through finished walls, are cleared continuously by gravity. Mineral precipitations and rust drop down and collect in the horizontal pipes below. These generally run through an unfinished basement or crawl space, where they are accessible.

Defective piping can be replaced by new pipes of identical material, but if your building code allows, it may be better to make new installations with durable plastic or copper piping. Plastic is far cheaper and easier to work with than steel. Copper, though more expensive, is lighter than steel and lasts longer.

To splice plastic or copper pipe into a steel system, you need one or two of the transition fittings shown at right. Once you install such fittings, you can join all the new piping together with standard couplings designed for that type of pipe.

Larger transition fittings are available to splice sections of plastic pipe into a cast-iron drainage system. But if you have only a short section of drainpipe to replace, it might be more convenient to use cast-iron piping with special couplings known as no-hub fittings *(page 80)*. Before you cut into a heavy vertical drainpipe, make sure it is supported above. In most cases, such a plumbing stack is attached to horizontal branch drains that are anchored to the house structure. However, if you must cut into a vent pipe that goes straight up through the roof and has no fixtures or branch piping, secure it with a pipe clamp braced by 2-by-4s, above the place where you will cut.

Unlike steel or cast-iron pipe, lead pipe is joined without fittings. Replacing lead pipe is a task for a professional. The job calls for elaborate joining techniques—which include wiping hot solder onto a pipe with a cloth—that should not be attempted by an amateur.

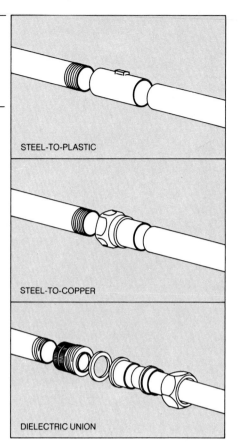

STEEL-TO-PLASTIC

STEEL-TO-COPPER

DIELECTRIC UNION

Three fittings. These couplings make it possible to graft pipes of new materials to old. A steel-to-plastic fitting consists of a short plastic tube with interior threads at one end to screw onto the existing steel pipe and a smooth bore at the other end for cementing to unthreaded plastic pipe A steel-to-copper adapter is similar, but is made of brass so the copper pipe can be soldered into the smooth end.

A more expensive copper-to-steel fitting, called a dielectric union, is better for permanent repairs. It consists of a threaded steel connector that fits the steel pipe, a copper connector for the copper pipe, a steel lock nut that clamps the two connectors, and a plastic ring and a neoprene washer that separate the two metals and prevent galvanic corrosion, which can occur between dissimilar metals.

Where steel pipe is so deteriorated that the fitting must be hacksawed off, use the slip fitting shown on page 76 to join two unthreaded pipes or to attach a threaded nipple that will join any of the other transition fittings. All of the fittings except the dielectric union are available straight, as shown, or in elbow or T configurations.

Four Ways to Connect Pipes

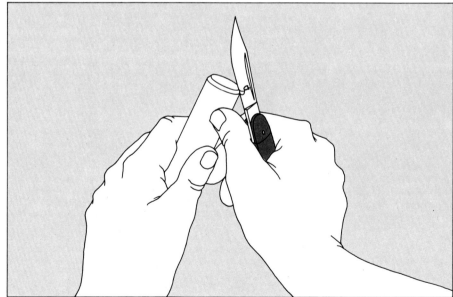

Cementing a plastic connector. Use a pocket knife to bevel the outside of the plastic pipe end slightly so that it will not push the cement from the joint. Paint a thick coat of the correct cement for the type of plastic pipe you are using around the outside of the pipe and a thinner coat on its end. Push the pipe into the plastic fitting and twist the parts to spread the cement evenly. Enough cement should be forced out of the fitting so that a smooth bead will form around the joint. If this does not happen, pull the pipe and fitting apart immediately—the cement will harden within seconds. Apply a thicker coat of cement and join the parts again.

Soldering a copper connector. Scour the inside of the fitting with a wire brush and, with emery cloth, sand the outside of the pipe as far as it will go into the fitting. Dry the pipes and fittings thoroughly. Apply a thin coat of soldering flux to both surfaces with a small brush. Slip the copper pipe into the connector and heat the pipe fitting with a propane torch. When both the fitting and the pipe are hot enough to melt the solder on contact, remove the torch and touch the solder to the joint between the two. Feed solder into the joint until a bead appears around the rim. Whenever possible, do the soldering on a workbench that is protected by an asbestos pad. If you must solder pipes in place, near the wood framing of the house, tape an asbestos pad behind the work and keep a fire extinguisher handy.

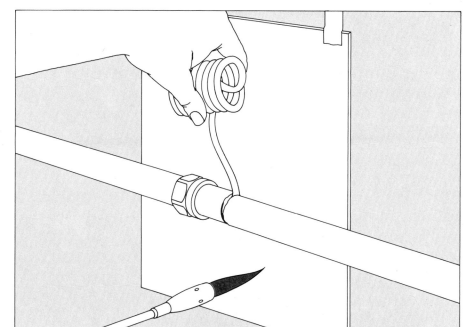

Installing a dielectric union. Slide the lock nut and plastic ring well up onto the copper pipe and solder the copper connector to the end of the pipe. After the connector has cooled, screw the steel connector onto the end of the steel pipe. Place the neoprene washer between the steel and copper connectors, then tighten the lock nut while holding the steel pipe with a second wrench to keep it from turning (*right*).

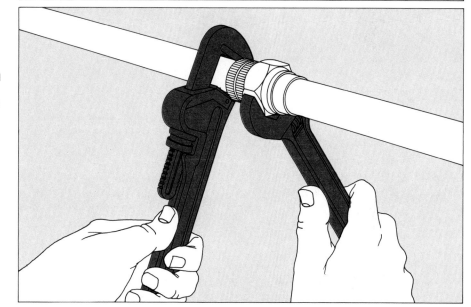

Installing a slip fitting. After cutting off the old threaded fitting with a hacksaw, or cutting through a badly rusted section, slip a lock nut from one end of the slip fitting over the stub of the old pipe. Fit the rubber washer inside the metal one and slide them onto the stub, with the metal washer adjoining the lock nut. Screw the lock nut down over the washer and onto the threaded end of the fitting. Attach a nipple to the other end of the fitting to accommodate any of the screw-on fittings shown opposite.

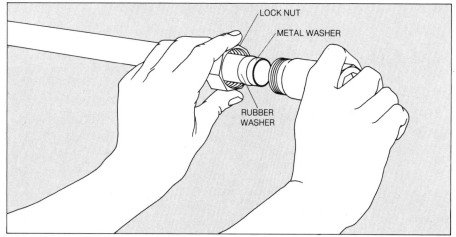

LOCK NUT

METAL WASHER

RUBBER WASHER

Replacing a Section of Cast-iron Pipe

1 Cutting the iron pipe. Wrap the chain of a pipe cutter around the pipe and tighten the knob that holds the cutter in place. Then work the tool back and forth until the pipe separates. Cut through the pipe above and below the damaged section and pull the cut piece out. Stuff toilet tissue into the lower cut end of the stack to prevent sewer gas from escaping. Use the pipe cutter to cut a new section of pipe ½ inch shorter than the distance between the cut ends.

2 Replacing the pipe section. Slip the flexible neoprene sleeves of a no-hub fitting over the cut ends of the existing pipe and slide the steel clamping straps onto the new section of pipe. Then fold the sleeves back onto themselves, push the new section of pipe into place and unfold the sleeves to cover the joints.

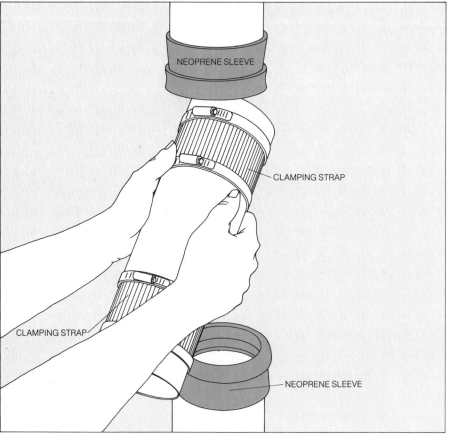

NEOPRENE SLEEVE

CLAMPING STRAP

CLAMPING STRAP

NEOPRENE SLEEVE

3 **Assembling the joint.** Slide the steel straps over the neoprene sleeves. Tighten the straps with a socket wrench or with the special plumber's T-handled torque-wrench socket tool illustrated at right. After a week, check the joint and retighten the clamps if necessary.

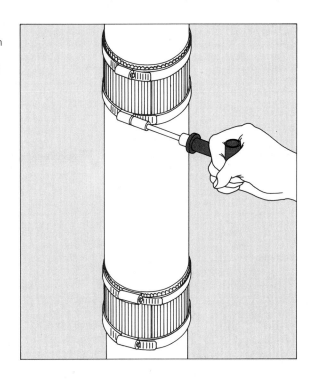

Making the Drains Flow Freely

Generally, a clogged drain can be unblocked easily with a plunger, a plumber's auger or even a bent coat hanger. But if all the fixtures drain slowly, chances are the main drain is clogged by tree roots.

To open the drains, rent a power auger and ream out the main drainpipe. Remove the cleanout plug at the base of the plumbing stack. If it cannot be turned with a large wrench, squirt penetrating oil around it and tap it lightly with a hammer, then try again.

Wearing gloves and safety goggles, push the sharp, root-cutting head of the tool well down into the pipe. Have a helper turn on the machine. Then, with the helper at the switch in case the head becomes jammed, feed the auger slowly into the drain. If the auger kicks, back it out about a foot, then work it in again. When it finally hits an obstruction that no amount of work will clear, withdraw it; you probably have reached the sewer main.

Replace the plug. Run water to wash out the root cuttings.

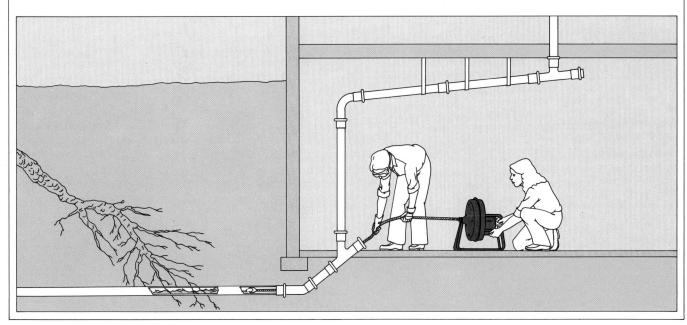

How to Live Safely with Old-fashioned Wiring

Old wiring that is unable to keep up with what is today a normal array of electrical equipment—kitchen appliances, heating and cooling units, laundry machines and power tools—should be upgraded or replaced as soon as possible. However, if you observe the cautionary instructions at right and on these and the following pages, you can in most cases get old wiring to provide safe and useful service until you are ready to improve it.

Follow a methodical course in determining the safety and adequacy of your wiring system. Look in the basement and other places where wiring is exposed to see if your house has knob-and-tube wiring—separate wires running between white knob insulators—or cable wiring, with all wires sheathed in metal or plastic. You can assume that a knob-and-tube installation is quite old and should be replaced at the earliest opportunity. If you need to use knob-and-tube wiring temporarily, at least make sure the insulation has not cracked or frayed.

A cable can be either of two types: armored cable, with a flexible metal jacket enclosing individually insulated wires; or nonmetallic cable, which can be either the modern, plastic-sheathed kind or its fabric-wrapped predecessor. With either type of cable, check the wires inside outlet and junction boxes; if the insulation is crumbling, it is wise to have a megohm test performed by an electrician. In this test, the wires in each circuit are disconnected at one end and current at 500 volts is fed into the wires at the other end. If the test indicates any shorts in the circuit, or that some of the current is passing through the insulation between the wires, the insulation is faulty and the circuit must be rewired.

Some houses have surface-mounted wiring in the form of light, rectangular metal raceways, heavier tubular metal conduit, or flat, wood moldings. As long as the insulation around the wires is sound, such wiring in most cases is safe. Wood moldings, however, provide little protection and should be replaced.

If the insulation around wires is good, the next potential problem to check is the number and capacity of the circuits. Since each circuit is protected by a fuse (or possibly by a more modern, switchlike circuit breaker) located in the main service panel or in subsidiary panels, you can count the circuits by counting the fuses or circuit breakers. The more circuits you have, the easier it will be to live with the installation *(page 18)*.

The capacity of a circuit is determined by the thickness of its wire and is guarded by a fuse that prevents more current from entering the circuit than its wires are capable of carrying. Excessive current would cause the wire to heat up, burn or melt the insulation and, in extreme cases, cause a fire. Make sure each fuse has the right rating for its circuit by measuring the wire thickness of the circuit *(opposite)* and matching the fuse rating to it.

For added safety, replace each old-fashioned fuse—the kind with a threaded base similar to that of a light bulb—with a threaded adapter. The adapter will accept only a special tamper-proof Type S fuse, preventing an over-sized fuse with a higher rating from being substituted for the correct one.

If your fuses blow frequently, map all the circuits in the house by removing the fuses one at a time and observing which outlets, fixtures and devices are affected. Add the wattage—printed or stamped on devices or bulbs—connected to each circuit and divide by 110 to estimate amperes. Compare these figures to the amperage of the fuse on each circuit. Redistribute the loads from heavily used circuits to lightly used ones and, if need be, label overloaded receptacles with warnings, such as, "Do not use toaster and electric skillet at the same time."

Check the condition of receptacles, switches and light fixtures. Receptacles that spark, get warm or no longer hold a plug tightly should be replaced. Receptacles in the floor can accumulate a surprising amount of dust; shut off the current at the fuse box, remove the covers from the receptacles and vacuum them.

If you have armored cable, conduit or raceway joined directly to the service panel or to outlet boxes wired with armored cable, the system probably has circuit grounding, a highly desirable feature. A grounded circuit contains an extra path through which current can pass safely to the service panel and its grounding bar, blowing a fuse in the event of trouble. If such a path of continuous enveloping metal—raceway or the spiral jacket of armored cable—is maintained throughout the circuit, you can replace old two-prong outlets with modern grounded, three-prong ones; new outlets are not expensive and the safety they provide is well worth the cost. But first have an electrician perform a ground-continuity test to make certain that the grounding connections have not become loose or corroded over the years.

Balky switches should also be replaced. Replacing a two-way switch is relatively easy. But replacing a three-way switch—part of a circuit in which a light fixture can be operated from two locations—requires special care, because two separate circuits may have been used.

Finally, note the number and locations of receptacles, light fixtures and switches. If your circuits have adequate capacity, you can add new devices on wall and ceiling surfaces by using metal raceway along the surfaces or by running new cable within the walls and ceilings.

While the procedures shown on these pages are recognized nationally as good practice, local codes vary from community to community. Check with local officials to determine if any special requirements apply to the work you plan to do.

Essential Safeguards to Protect against Shocks

Electric shock is always dangerous and can be fatal. Before working on any electrical device, you must make sure that no current is flowing in or near it. The surest way to check is with a voltage tester. This inexpensive tool (below) consists of a small neon bulb and two leads tipped with metal probes.

Before working in any electrical box, remove the fuse or switch off the circuit breaker that protects the circuit. Then, to be doubly sure you have cut off the correct circuit, touch the probes of the voltage tester to every combination of wires, terminals and parts of the box. If the bulb glows, current is still reaching the box. Find the correct fuse and remove it; if you cannot, call an electrician.

Protect yourself further by following these additional safety rules:
☐ Never touch any plumbing pipes or gas lines while you work with electricity. Make sure the floor is dry, or stand on a piece of dry plywood.
☐ Label the service panel with a notice so that no one will restore power to a circuit while you are working.
☐ Check your finished work with the power on. The voltage tester should glow when one of the leads is touched to an unswitched black wire and the other is touched to a white or bare wire or a part of the metal box. The tester should not glow on any combination of parts that does *not* include a black or red wire.

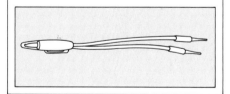

A knob-and-tube installation. Knob-and-tube wiring gets its name from the porcelain insulating knobs that support runs of wire and the porcelain tubes that carry wires through holes in beams. The wires, with cloth-covered rubber insulation, in most cases were run in pairs—the hot, electrically charged wire is black and the neutral wire is white except in early installations, in which both the hot and neutral are black. Early codes mandated a separation of at least 2½ inches between the wires; where they needed to be closer to enter a box, they were surrounded with fabric tubing called loom.

Examine the wires for deteriorating insulation. If the original installation has been compromised by improvised attempts to extend circuits, shut off the power and remove any substandard additions—that is, those whose wires run less than 2½ inches apart, are undersized or dangling.

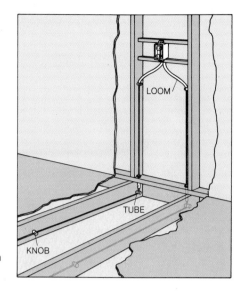

Matching the Wires and the Fuses

1 **Checking the wire size.** Identify the wire size used for each circuit, to determine the appropriate fuse size for that circuit. Shut off the power and remove an outlet from its box in the wall; unscrew one of the wires at its side. Measure with a wire gauge, or by comparison with short sample lengths from an electrical-parts supplier. Profiles of the three most common gauges of house-circuit wire are shown in the inset.

A circuit of No. 14 wire requires a 15-ampere fuse; No. 12 wire a 20-ampere fuse; No. 10 wire a 30-ampere fuse. Ratings are higher in most local codes for knob-and-tube wiring because the wires, surrounded by air, stay cooler: No. 14 wire can have a 20-ampere fuse; No. 12 wire a 25-ampere fuse, and No. 10 wire a 40-ampere fuse. However, if your knob-and-tube system has smaller-capacity fuses, do not upgrade them.

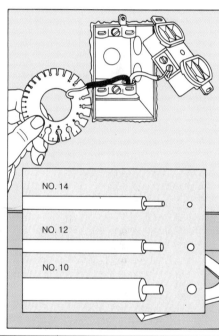

2 **Installing tamper-proof fuses.** Thread a tamper-proof adapter onto a Type S fuse of the size required for each circuit (inset). Then screw the fuse-and-adapter assembly into the fuse socket for that circuit. The adapters make it impossible to use a fuse of the wrong rating.

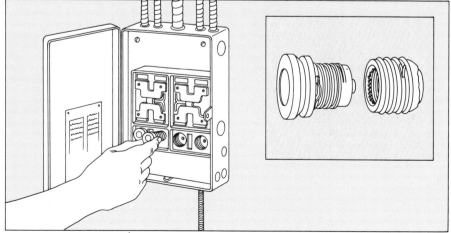

Renewing Outlets and Switches

Tightening up on armored cable. The spiral metal jacket of armored cable provides a continuous ground connection to all electrical boxes. If the jacket has come free of the clamp that holds it to the box, you can restore the box's ground contact by turning off the power, loosening the box clamp, carefully pulling the cable back into the box and tightening the clamp. If the clamp is located outside of the box, you must make a hole in the wall to reach it; be sure the nut that holds the external clamp from inside the box is tight. At the end of each cable you should see a red insulating sleeve that prevents the cut edge of the metal from slicing into the wire insulation. If the sleeve is missing, try to slip one around the wires and into the cable end.

Repairing cracked insulation. If the insulation of a wire in a box has deteriorated or crumbles when touched, the whole circuit should be rewired. There is a chance you can save it, but only if the damage does not extend all the way to the point where the wire leaves the box. With the power off, strip the deteriorated insulation from its wire. Strip a matching length of insulation from a new wire that is one size larger than the wire in the box *(below, top)*. Then slip the new insulation over the bare wire *(below, bottom)*. Tape the joint with enough electrical tape to equal the thickness of the original insulation.

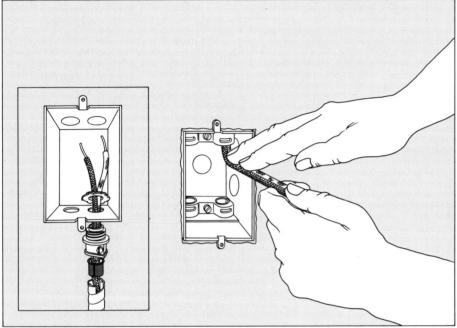

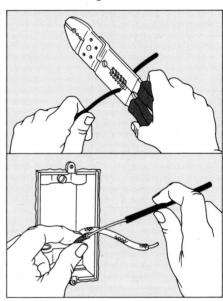

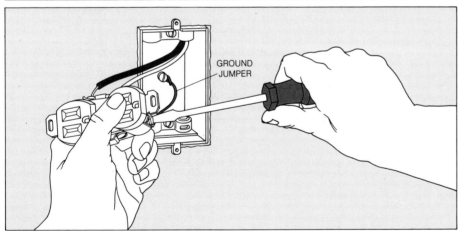

GROUND JUMPER

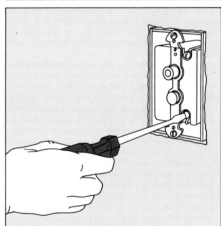

Replacing a receptacle. If your house is wired with armored cable, local codes may require that if you replace a defective ungrounded two-slot receptacle, you do so with a three-slot grounded unit. Turn off power to the circuit, remove the cover plate and pull the old receptacle out of the box. Unscrew the wires from the receptacle and screw them to the new receptacle; the white wire goes to the silver terminal, and the black goes to the brass terminal. To add the ground connection, screw a ground jumper—a piece of bare wire with one end looped around a screw —to the box and to the green terminal on the receptacle. To be sure the new receptacle is adequately grounded, have an electrician perform a ground-continuity test.

Some outlet boxes have a cable from the power source and one leading on to another box. Connect the two white wires of such a pair of cables to the silver terminals of the receptacle and the two black wires to the brass terminals.

Replacing a switch. Shut off power to the old switch, remove the cover plate, and pull the switch from the box. Attach the wires to the terminals of a new switch in the same way they were attached to the old. Take care to orient a toggle switch so that the words "on" and "off" are upright. If you are replacing a push-button switch with a toggle switch, you will need a new cover plate. If the old switch has three terminals, it is part of a three-way circuit; follow the procedures on the opposite page.

Rewiring Three-way Switches

A regular household switch that turns a light fixture on or off from a single location is a straightforward device. It has only two terminals and simply permits or blocks the passage of current between a power source and a fixture. Three-way switches, those that turn a light on and off from two locations, have three terminals instead of two and contain a mechanism that directs the current along any of several paths.

The modern method of wiring three-way switches ensures that all the switching takes place along the current-carrying hot wires. However, some old houses have three-way circuits in which both the hot and the neutral wires are connected to the switches and the light is turned off or on by an interruption in either the hot or the neutral wire. This early installation was used because it was generally easier to do and sometimes required less wire. The method was abandoned when a rule was inserted in the National Electrical Code forbidding the interruption of a neutral wire.

No matter which wiring scheme your three-way switches follow, the procedure for replacing them is the same: Connect the common wire—the one that is connected to the common terminal of the switch—to the new common terminal and connect the traveler wires to the traveler terminals.

First turn off the power at the service panel and check the switch box carefully with a voltage tester (page 83); since power in a three-way system follows variable paths, the wires may be live even though the light fixture is off. Then, if the switch is coded—most have a dark screw for the common and lighter ones for the travelers—simply duplicate the old wiring pattern when you attach the wires to the new switch.

If the terminals of the switch are not coded, you can, with the power off, use an inexpensive device called a continuity tester to identify the terminals. The tester has a metal probe at one end, a wire with an alligator clip at the other, and a battery and bulb inside; if the clip and the probe are touched to terminals that are connected inside a switch, the tester bulb will light.

To test a three-way switch, turn off the power and disconnect the switch, taking care to label each wire so you can later tell which one was attached to which terminal. Then find the pair of terminals that will not light the tester bulb regardless of the position of the switch toggle. These are the traveler terminals; the remaining one is the common terminal.

If another combination of terminals also fails to light the tester bulb, the switch is defective. If your other switch is identical, perform the continuity test on it to find the common terminal. If your switches are not identical, have an electrician identify the terminals.

Modern three-way switching. The hot wire from the house wiring is connected to the common terminal of the first (left) switch. A pair of traveler wires is connected to the traveler terminals, passed through the light-fixture box and attached to the traveler terminals of the second switch. Another wire runs from the common terminal of the second switch to a lead from the light fixture; a neutral wire connected to the other lead from the fixture completes the circuit.

In a variation on this wiring layout, the light fixture is wired beyond the switches rather than between them. Electrically, the wiring is the same; the second switch, however, will have two wires passing unconnected through its box.

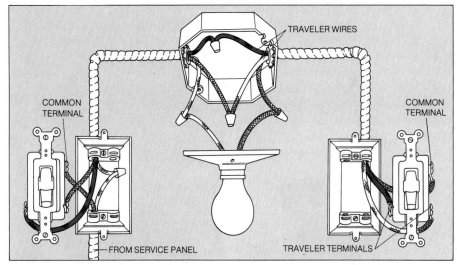

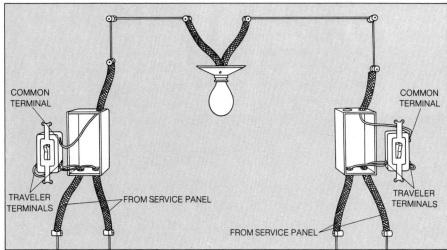

Old-fashioned three-way switching. In this switch-wiring method, which was often employed in knob-and-tube installations and occasionally used in armored-cable installations, hot wires are connected to one of the traveler terminals of each switch. The corresponding neutral wires from the house line are connected to the other traveler terminal of each switch. A single wire runs from the common terminal of each switch to the leads of the light fixture.

Adding On with Surface Wiring

Even if the wiring in your house has adequate capacity, you may still find that you do not have enough outlets. If you have circuits with extra capacity, it is a fairly simple matter to add new outlets to an old system by running new wiring inside new surface-mounted raceway or within the old walls. You can also use such new runs of wire to install a wall switch for an overhead lighting fixture that has only a pull-chain switch.

Raceway wiring systems include a wide variety of pieces that allow you to lead the raceway out from a wall box or lighting fixture, along walls and around corners. To be sure of getting all of the various pieces you will need, make a sketch of your intended installation before going to the electrical-supply store.

A variety of components. Raceway parts fall into three groups. First are the devices with open back plates, such as the overhead-fixture box and the outlet-adapter box shown here, that join raceway systems onto existing ceiling or wall boxes. Next are the devices with solid back plates.

such as the switch and outlet boxes shown here, that terminate new runs. Finally there are the components that allow you to lead wiring from one box to another, such as straight runs of raceway (these are available in 5- and 10-foot sections) and cornering brackets.

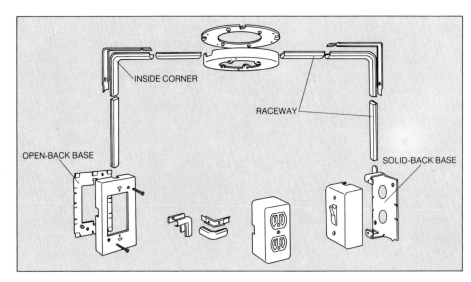

Installing Raceway for a Wall Switch

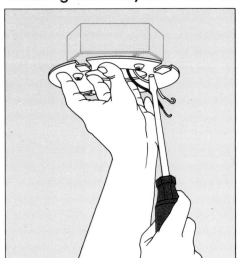

1 Extending from a ceiling box. Shut off the power, remove the light fixture from the ceiling box and unscrew the wire caps that secure the fixture wires to the wires in the box. Loosely mount the base of the adapter box on the ceiling box with screws. Rotate the base plate so that one of the tongues, used to support the end of a raceway run, will point in the appropriate direction; tighten the screws.

2 Running the raceway. Insert an inside corner base into the end of a section of raceway, hold the raceway against the ceiling between the wall-ceiling corner and the base of the adapter box and mark the raceway where it meets the appropriate tongue on the adapter base. Cut the raceway with a hacksaw, slip the cut end over the box tongue and screw the inside corner base to the ceiling.

For long runs of raceway, fasten clips to the ceiling along the path of the raceway and snap the raceway into the clips (inset). Install the fixture-adapter cover after first removing a breakaway tab from it to receive the raceway.

Cut the raceway for a run down the wall to the desired switch location, insert the ends over the tongues of the corner base and the switch-box base, and screw the switch-box base to the wall.

Push a pair of black wires through the raceway to the fixture adapter, install a switch onto the switch-box base, connect the wires to the switch and install the switch-box cover. Using wire caps, connect the white wire of the ceiling box to the white wire of the fixture. Connect one switch wire to the black wire of the box, and the other to the black wire of the fixture. Screw the fixture to the adapter. If necessary, notch the fixture base to receive the raceway.

Installing Cable
for a New Outlet

1 **Running a new cable.** Remove 6 inches of
sheathing from the end of a plastic-sheathed
cable and, using a cable clamp, fasten the cable
inside a convenient basement outlet box to
which the power has been shut off or, if your
house has no basement, to an attic junction
box nearest the point where the supply cable enters the attic. Inside the outlet box, connect the
white wire of the new cable to an unused silver-
colored screw on the receptacle and connect
the black wire to a brass screw. With a wire cap,
join the ground wire of the new cable to a
ground jumper wire connected to a grounding
screw in the box. If the existing receptacle is
not grounded, substitute a three-slot receptacle
and add a ground jumper to connect the green
terminal of the receptacle with the grounding
screw of the box.

To make a connection inside a junction box,
join the black, white and grounding wires of the
new cable with their respective counterparts,
using wire caps (inset). Fasten the new cable
along a basement joist or attic rafter with cable staples straddling the cable, until you can feed
it inside a wall to the location of the new outlet
box. Using the same techniques, you can tap into
an existing first-floor outlet box and run a
cable through the basement to a new outlet box
elsewhere, though you may need to make a
hole in the wall near the old outlet box to do so. Or
you can run a cable from an existing box up
through the attic for a new outlet box upstairs.

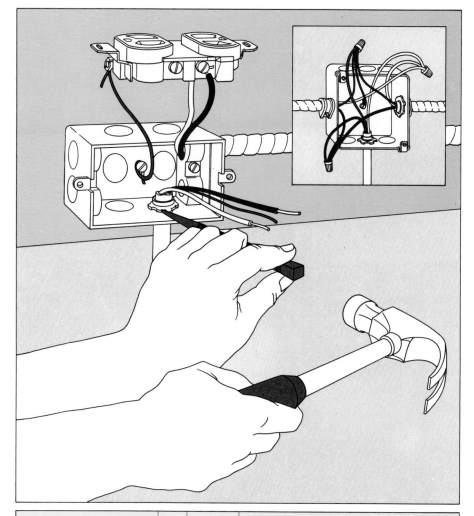

2 **Adding a box.** With a stud locator, find a stud
near where you would like to put the new box.
Drill a hole next to the stud and enlarge it with a
keyhole or saber saw to match the outline of
the box. Run the new cable inside the wall from
the basement or attic to the hole, strip the insulation from the end of the cable and clamp it to
the box. Slip the box into the hole and toenail
it to the side of the stud, or hold it snugly in place
with brackets made for this purpose. You can
then add a receptacle or light fixture or use the
box as a starting point for raceway.

A wide variety of boxes, in different sizes and
equipped with any of several kinds of brackets,
clamps and flanges allows new outlet boxes to
be installed almost anywhere along a wall, baseboard or floor, or even outdoors.

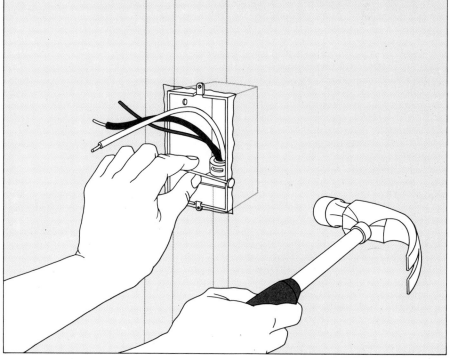

First Aid for Structural Faults

Giving the floor a boost. Like a cast-iron Atlas, a deceptively small, bell-shaped screw jack capable of lifting a house weighing many tons presses upward against a strong wooden beam under floor joists. When the jack has lifted the floor a fraction of an inch, it can be replaced by a vertical wooden post to hold the position while the jack lifts another section.

The structural faults of an old house are seldom as threatening as they seem when you first notice them. Of course, all major flaws require fixing, but many can wait years, if necessary, for repair. A floor may sag, a rafter may weaken or a foundation may stand cracked for decades without threatening the overall stability of a house. Only a small minority of structural defects, such as a termite infestation or a roofing leak, demand immediate attention.

When you do address a structural problem, understanding that the structure of an old house is something special is the first step toward repairing it. People accustomed to the highly standardized houses of today are often surprised by their first careful look at the skeleton that supports an old house. Many old foundations, for example, do not have footings, the concrete pads underneath the foundation that are universally required today to distribute the weight of a house. Until the early 19th Century, when portland cement was invented, mortar was a weak mix of sand and lime, the lime obtained by crushing and burning oyster shells. Nothing but gravity held the exterior walls of many wood-frame houses to their foundations because there were no steel anchor bolts to attach the walls to the sills.

Concrete blocks, now the most common material used to build foundation walls, were almost unknown until 1900; granite, brick, fieldstone and structural clay tile were dominant. The first concrete blocks were made on the building site in a hand-operated molding machine. People were so suspicious of the new material that in 1921 the Concrete Products Association had to set a concrete-block house afire to prove to insurance companies that the blocks were more fire-resistant than wood and deserved a better fire rating.

Yet some of the structural features of old houses are superior to those used today. The masonry walls are often massive, as much as 24 inches thick in some houses. Wood framing members are usually much thicker and stronger, and in very old houses are locked together by mortise-and-tenon joints instead of nails. (Labor to make the joints was cheap; nails were scarce and expensive.) Wall studs, because they were usually twice as thick, could be spaced farther apart—in some houses as much as 28 inches—compared with the standard 16 inches set in the early 1900s.

Despite these advantages, old wooden houses are just as vulnerable to rot, stress, weather and termite infestation as modern houses and, because of their age, are more apt to have these problems. Solid-masonry houses, which are less flexible, show their age in crumbling mortar and structural cracks. But in other ways time has left old houses strong, and many of them lack only a new rafter or a batch of fresh mortar to make them whole again.

The Roof: Finding and Fixing Small Leaks

The simplest roof problems to detect and remedy—and problems that potentially endanger all other systems in the house—are leaks in the broad expanse of the roof itself. Only a bit harder to find and fix are leaks under flashing—the metal strips that seal the joints where roof slopes converge or where the roof meets a wall or chimney—or in gutters that channel water away from the house.

In the roof, it is usually easy to spot asphalt shingles that are torn, worn or curled, or wood shingles, slates or tiles that are rotted, cracked or missing altogether. Here, unless the damage is so severe that complete reroofing is required, it is best to confine repairs to simple but immediate fixes of small areas—one or two damaged units. Trying to patch up a larger area can disturb the interdependent anatomy of a roof's structure and cause more problems than are solved.

Leaks in more vulnerable places, such as the valleys between roof slopes and the joints between the roof and chimneys, dormer walls, pipes and vents, are harder to pinpoint. Examine flashing to see that it is unbroken and has edges properly sealed; roofing cement seals best on most roofs. From inside an unfinished attic, look for daylight and mark where it enters by poking a wire through.

Even if a roof is waterproof, problems will arise if the gutters fail to do their job efficiently. Clean out any debris, then spray the roof with a hose and watch the gutters for pooling—a symptom of sag or other misalignment. Look for rust in metal gutters and rot in wooden ones. Small spots of rust or rot can be patched with fiberglass *(page 97)* or with an inside coat of roofing cement, but if large sections are damaged, replace them.

If you wish to preserve the historic look of wooden gutters, you can order new ones made at a mill, or move a sound section from a less conspicuous part of your house. Otherwise, metal gutters are the most practical and readily available substitute. Made in a variety of shapes, they provide the simplest way to add gutters to a house that has none but needs them—and they are definitely needed if the eave overhang is too narrow to keep water from draining down onto the walls of the house.

Sometimes a roof problem is not in the exterior armor but in the skeletal structure beneath. You can brace a sagging ridge beam if a bearing wall is directly below it, or transfer some of the roof load from the rafters to the joists beneath. Either technique may cause hairline cracks in plaster below but will arrest further settling. Another simple way to reinforce a roof is to install new "sister"

rafters and joists, cut the same size as the old counterparts and nailed to them.

Once you have determined what repairs your roof requires, gather the materials and tools you need. There is a special slate puller, for instance, that is handy for cutting nails concealed beneath wood shingles, slates or tiles. Roofing cement, liquid roof coating and metal flashing may all be on your shopping list. New flashing is available in copper, aluminum, zinc or galvanized steel; match the kind you already have to avoid the possibility of galvanic corrosion, which sometimes occurs if dissimilar metals touch each other.

Finally, always be careful when you work on a roof. Make sure it is completely dry, and wear nonslip shoes. Let professionals do the work on extremely steep roofs. Except on flat roofs or the shallowest of pitches, use a climbing support such as an extension ladder stabilized with ladder hooks caught over the ridge. Alternatively, a 1-by-12 board with horizontal cleats—called a chicken ladder—improves your footing and distributes your weight on slippery, brittle slates and tiles when it is anchored securely at the peak with ladder hooks; and a projecting stabilizer can be used to keep a ladder set on the ground from leaning against gutters while you work on them.

Restoring Damaged Pieces

Mending a torn shingle. Spread a thin coating of roofing cement under a damaged asphalt shingle, press the flaps flat and drive galvanized roofing nails along each side of the tear. Cover the nailheads and the tear with roofing cement.

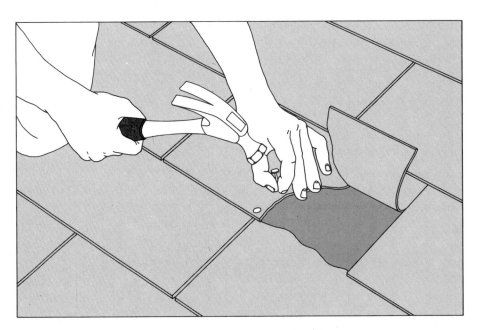

Patching a broken shingle with metal. To prevent a leak from developing through a crack in a wood shingle or a slate, cut a piece of metal flashing that is twice the width and 3 inches longer than the exposed part of the damaged shingle. Spread roofing cement on one side of the flashing and slide it under the broken shingle and the adjacent shingles, cemented side down. Use a wood block and a hammer to tap the flashing in until its upper edge extends past the lower edges of the shingles in the course above.

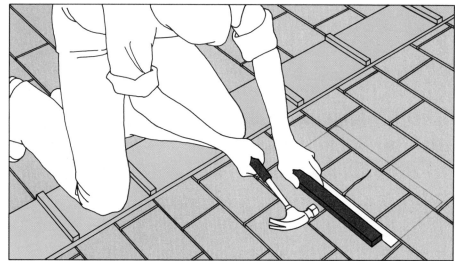

Coating pitted or pinholed metal. Use a roofer's mop or a stiff-bristled push broom to brush roof coating—a thick, asphalt-based liquid—on a pitted metal roof or along damaged flashing. Work the coating well into all valleys and joints.

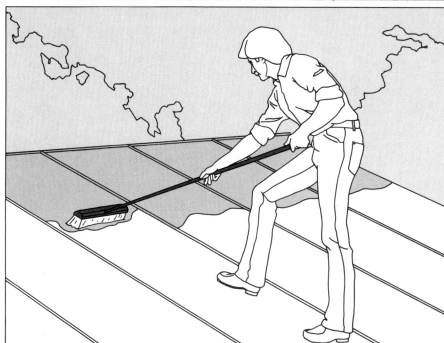

Resetting flashing in a mortar joint. If flashing is loose where it joins a masonry wall or chimney, pull it out of the way and clean the old mortar out of the entire joint to a depth of 1½ inches, using a cold chisel or a brickset. Refill the joint with roofing cement, push the lip of the flashing back into it, and drive a masonry nail near the top of the mortar joint so that it wedges the flashing in place (inset). Do not pierce the flashing with the nail. When you have secured the flashing, seal the metal-to-masonry joint with a 2-inch-wide coating of roofing cement.

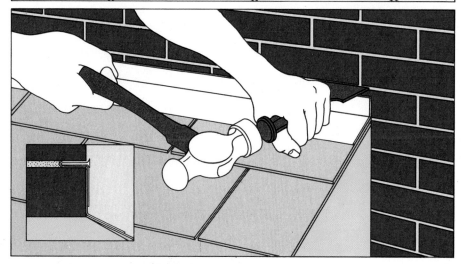

Replacing Damaged Pieces

Removing broken remnants. Slide the arrow-shaped head of a slate puller under a broken slate, wood shingle or clay tile and hook an end notch around a nail. Cut the nail with a sharp hammer blow on the raised handle of the slate puller. If you do not have a slate puller, wear gloves and use a long hacksaw blade to cut the nails. The nails holding tiles are located along the flat section of the tile *(inset)*.

After cutting the nails, slide out the broken piece without disturbing adjacent slates or tiles.

Securing a replacement slate. Cut a holding tab, a 2-inch-wide strip of metal flashing that is long enough to extend several inches under the course above, and about an inch below, the replacement slate. Nail it to the roof through the joint in the course that underlies the replacement *(below, left)*. Coat the nailheads with roofing cement, slide the new slate into position and bend the projecting holding tab up and over the bottom edge of the new slate *(below, right)*.

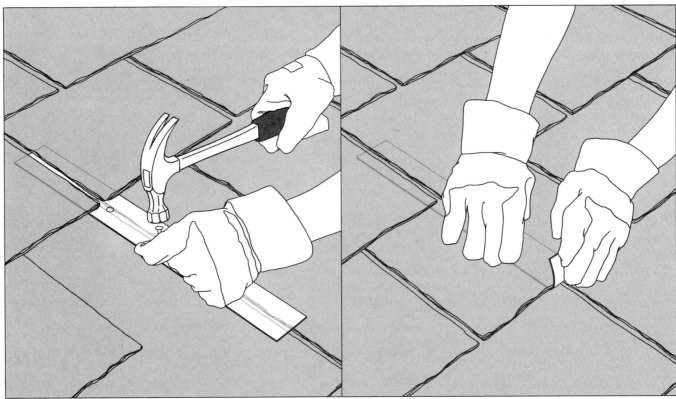

Replacing a tile. Nail a holding tab like the one used for a slate (*opposite*) to the roof where the flat part of the new tile will rest. Put dabs of roofing cement over the nailheads and underneath the tile in the overlying course, where the edges of the new tile will slide. Then slide the new tile into position; bend the holding tab up and round its bottom edge.

Replacing a wood shingle. After removing all the remnants of the damaged shingle—splitting it with a chisel if necessary—use a hammer and wood block to tap a new shingle into position. Cut the replacement shingle ½ inch narrower than the space it will fill, to allow for expansion. If the shingle is too long, pull it out and trim the excess length from the thin end. When the shingle is in line with the others in its course, secure it with two galvanized roofing nails just below the edge of the overlying course. Cover the nailheads with roofing cement.

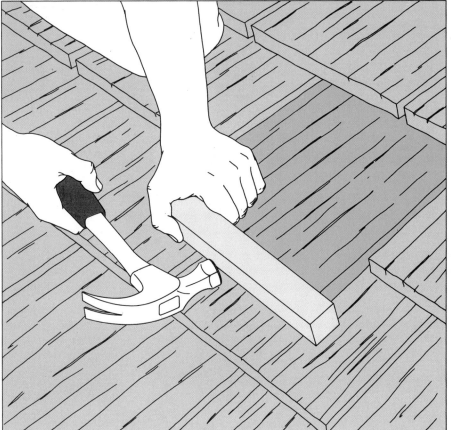

Protecting the Edges with Metal

Adding a drip edge. The fascia, a board running across the rafters at the eave, can rot if water soaks it. To protect it, slide the lip of a preformed metal drip edge between the roof sheathing and the shingles at the eave; drive roofing nails between the tabs of the first course of shingles through the underlying starter course and the drip edge, and into the sheathing (*below, left*).

Cover the nailheads with roofing cement and slide a 2-inch-wide strip of flashing over them, under the first course of shingles and slightly under the second (*below, right*).

If you then install a gutter as well, slide the back edge of the gutter behind the drip edge before securing the gutter to the fascia.

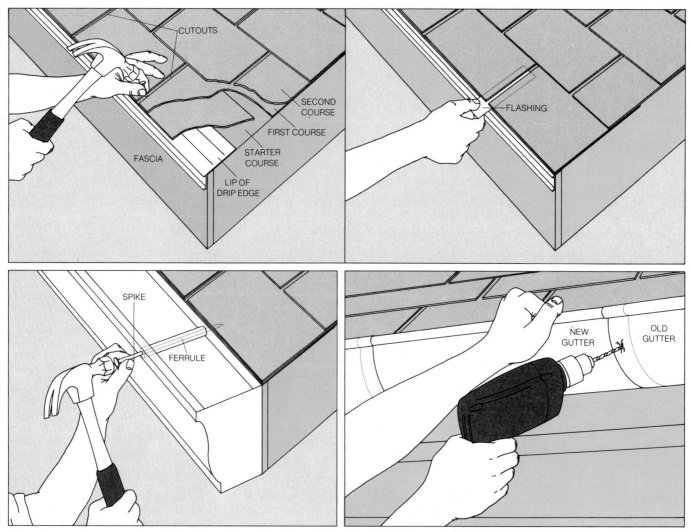

Taking the sag out of a gutter. If pooling of water indicates that a gutter has sagged out of alignment, remove the nails or brackets securing the sagging portion and reposition the gutter so it will drain. Secure it in place with a spike and ferrule; the latter is a tubelike spacer set inside the gutter. Drive the spike through the gutter, then through the ferrule and finally into each of the rafter ends. The rafters will be indicated by vertical lines of nailheads on the fascia.

Replacing a rusted gutter section. After using a hacksaw to cut away a gutter section that has rusted through, spread roofing cement inside the cut ends on each side of the opening, slip in a new piece of gutter long enough to rest on the cut ends, and drill at least four holes through the overlapping ends of the old and new gutter sections. Use a riveting tool to install pop rivets, or drive sheet-metal screws into the holes to secure the sections.

If the crimped front edges of the old and new sections do not fit tightly, use metal snips to cut the crimp off the ends of the new section.

Bracing the Roof Frame from inside the Attic

Installing rafter braces. To reinforce sagging rafters, install a 2-by-6 brace at a right angle to each rafter, down to the corresponding joist below. Nail one end of each 2-by-6 to the rafter, midway between the ridge and the eave. Then nail the other end to the side of the joist.

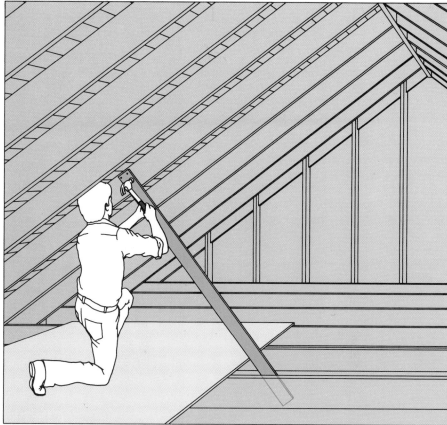

Strengthening the ridge beam. To brace a sagging ridge beam where there is a supporting wall under the attic floor directly below the ridge, install vertical 4-by-4 posts between a 2-by-4 top plate nailed to the underside of the ridge beam (or, if necessary, to the undersides of the rafters as shown in the inset) and a 2-by-4 bottom plate that runs directly below, across the joists. Measure the distance between the two plates and cut a 4-by-4 post that will fit tightly.

Rest one end of the post on the bottom plate directly over a joist, angle the top end against the top plate, and use a heavy mallet to tap the post into a vertical position. Use a level to make sure the post is plumb, then toenail it to the top and bottom plates. Install the remaining posts in the same way, spacing them every 8 to 10 feet along the length of the ridge.

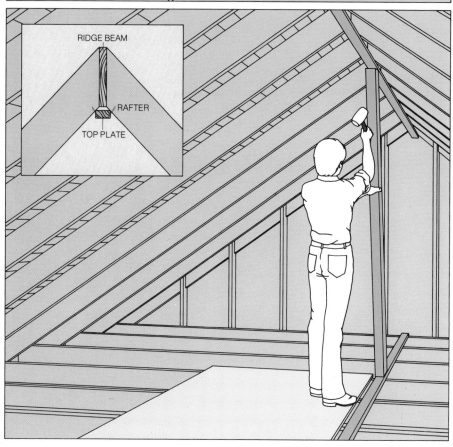

Bandaging Surface Cracks with Fiberglass

Deteriorated and damaged surfaces are ubiquitous in the old house. Inside it, years of settling and door slamming crack plaster. Outside, rain and sun chip away at concrete and stucco, rot wood and eat into metal. Traditionally, damage to these surfaces is repaired by filling or coating them with a like material: patching plaster for walls, mortar for masonry, a soldered patch for metal. But many homeowners have found fiberglass patches more effective for some of these repairs.

A patch of fiberglass is literally a bandage—a piece of tough cloth held to the skin of a roof, wall, gutter or sill with a sticky adhesive. Instead of filling cracks, it bridges them and, because it is waterproof and remains slightly pliable, it keeps the damage from recurring with the next rain or the next slam of a door.

While fiberglass patches can be used on practically any building material—they are applied the same way to any surface—you still may need traditional patching materials for some jobs. Fiberglass seldom matches the material it is applied to (the adhesive dries a muddy white) so it generally is used only in

places that will be painted or where appearance is unimportant. Deep holes must be filled before they can be bandaged and, because the adhesive and fiberglass remain pliable, such a patch cannot be used on floors or other walkways.

To make a fiberglass patch, you need the fabric and a special adhesive; both are stocked by many paint and hardware stores. The fabric, most commonly sold under the trade name Tuffglass, comes in 16- and 36-foot rolls that are 3¾, 5½, 11 or 22 inches wide. The patches can be overlapped for larger areas.

The adhesive, sold mostly under the trade name Tuff-Kote for exterior use and Krack-Kote for interior, comes in various sizes. A 1-quart can, enough to patch about 10 square feet, is ample for most household jobs. Made from soybean and linseed oils, the adhesive tends to separate on the shelf; stir well before use.

Along with the fabric and adhesive, you will generally get a free applicator—a light metal smoothing tool that resembles a slat from a venetian blind. While it will serve for small jobs, you may want to buy a special cornering tool or straight-

edged smoother if you plan to do a lot of patching. Both are sold with the fabric and adhesives, and resemble rubber-edged trowels. You also will need a paint brush 2½ inches or smaller to spread the adhesive (use a brush you can throw away—the adhesive is difficult to remove), a pair of scissors to cut the fabric and a supply of turpentine for cleaning up.

Before applying a fiberglass patch, make sure your surface is clean and dry. Scrape away any loose paint or, for metal, use a wire brush to remove rust or corrosion. Powdery surfaces, such as concrete or plaster, should be wiped with a damp rag. If they still feel dusty when dry, they need to be varnished. Extinguish nearby flames before opening the adhesive, and open windows if working indoors.

When patching, take care to apply the final coat of adhesive smoothly; unlike plaster, which dries hard, this material cannot be sanded smooth later. If you are patching concrete or stucco, stipple the final coat with a brush or textured roller to match the surrounding surface. The fiberglass patch can be painted after drying for 24 hours.

Patching a Flat Surface

1 Applying the adhesive. Paint the adhesive over the crack, spreading it evenly with smooth brushstrokes. Cover the crack and the wall around it to a width 2 inches greater than the width of your fabric and at least 1 inch beyond each end of the crack. Cut the fabric with scissors to the length of the crack plus 2 inches. With your fingers, press the fabric lightly onto the adhesive. If you find that you need more than one piece of fabric, lap the second piece at least 1½ inches over the edge of the first.

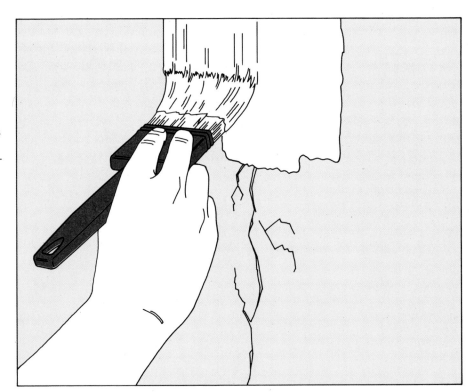

2 Embedding the fabric. Hold the applicator almost at a right angle to the wall, across the center of the fabric. Working out toward the ends, scrape the applicator over the fabric to push it well into the adhesive. Hold the applicator with both hands, thumbs underneath and fingers close together near the center, to keep it stiff. Keep the concave edge up as you sweep it downward; turn it over for upsweeps. After embedding the cloth, let the adhesive dry for two hours for interior patches, until it is tacky for exterior ones. In either case, brush on a second coat of adhesive.

3 Smoothing the final coat. Immediately after applying the second adhesive coat, grasp the applicator, with your fingers well away from the edge, and sweep it lightly out from the center to the sides of the patch. Go over the patch two or three times to smooth it and feather the edges of the adhesive. On textured surfaces, stipple the final coat with a brush or paint roller.

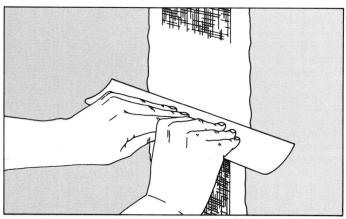

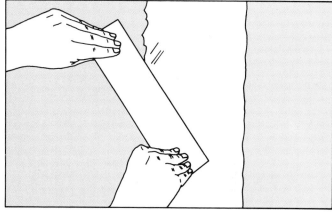

Special Techniques for Corners and Curves

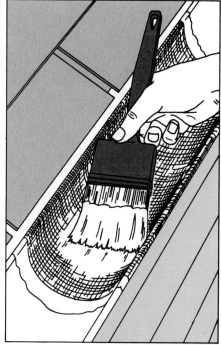

Patching an interior corner. After applying the adhesive, fold a single piece of the fabric and press it into the corner. Then embed the fabric with the point of a special cornering tool. First work up and down the corner, then smooth the fabric out toward the edges on each side.

Patching an exterior corner. After spreading the adhesive, stretch the fabric smoothly around the corner from one surface to the next. Embed the fabric by working from the corner out to the edges on both sides. Finally, feather the edges as you did in Step 3, above.

Patching a curved surface. For contours where the applicator cannot reach—the inside of a rusted gutter, for example—you can embed the fabric with a paint brush. Though the patch will not be as smooth as on a flat surface, it will seal tightly and weatherproof the surface.

Shielding the Outside from Moisture and Dirt

The exterior covering of a house has a double job—it must protect the structure and contents of the house from the elements, and it must protect itself. For masonry houses—brick, stone or stucco—resistance to the weather is built in; as long as bricks and mortar are intact, they will be weather-tight. Wood sidings, except for such naturally rot-resistant woods as cedar and redwood, must be painted to repel water.

Before you repaint the outside of a wood house, wash it down well with a garden hose, using a mild detergent and a scrub brush where the dirt is thick. Scrape off loose or peeling paint. Then give the surface a complete examination. Dark stains, blistering, cracking and rust streaks around nailheads all show that moisture is getting into the wood. Unless the source is tracked down and fixed, your new paint will not last.

If the damage is near a bathroom or kitchen, you may need a vent or exhaust fan to keep moist air from attacking the siding from inside. Make sure gutters are in good condition so they channel roof drainage away from the walls (page 94). Caulk liberally around windows, doors and any other interruptions in the wall surface; butyl or vinyl caulking lasts longest but sticks only to a well-cleaned crevice. Oil-base caulk is easiest to use since it can be applied over old caulk.

Once the walls are clean and sealed, any boards that have rotted through should be replaced (page 107). If the damage is slight, though, you can save a board by scraping it bare, letting it dry for several days, and treating it with wood preservative. Cracks and splits in boards can be filled with caulk or, if they are large, packed with oakum—hemp impregnated with oil—before caulking.

Masonry houses are generally easier to maintain than wood houses. Unless the walls are badly deteriorated, they generally need only to be repointed. Even cleaning is optional. Until recently masons believed that dirt and other pollutants on brick gradually ate into the surface. New research, however, suggests that in some cases grime can actually form a protective shell, and cleaning it off an old house can be harmful.

Old bricks are not uniformly hard. Because they were often unevenly fired in makeshift kilns, usually on the building site, the surfaces dried harder than the centers. If the surface of such a brick is damaged, the softer interior will pit or even crumble with exposure. Today's bricks are more uniform; still, take care not to damage their surfaces.

So if you wish to clean a brick house, do it gently. If flushing the walls with an ordinary garden hose works, then that is the method to use. If it does not, rent a pressure washer. Typically such a machine takes water from the house and jets it out of a nozzle at a pressure of 600 pounds per square inch, blasting off dirt.

The best models are adjustable for any pressure up to 1,000 pounds and have reservoirs to hold detergents or other chemicals that can be fed into the water stream as needed. If you use a pressure washer, choose the lowest pressure and the weakest chemical that will work.

If pressure washing fails to clean particularly dirty patches, scrape and brush them gingerly, or apply a commercial masonry-cleaning compound or dilute muriatic acid. Mix 1 part acid with 9 parts water (always adding the acid to the water). Wear rubber gloves and protective clothing, and use a long-handled stiff brush to apply the solution to damp bricks. Then flush the wall thoroughly with the pressure washer.

Only as a last resort should brick ever be sandblasted. This process seriously damages the surface and necessitates applying silicone or some other masonry-waterproofing compound to seal the wall—a tedious job that must be repeated, possibly every two years. Brick that shows pitting should be painted or, like sandblasted bricks, sealed with silicone.

Brick walls that have been painted should be repainted. Spills from painting trim can be taken off with a masonry paint remover containing an alkaline solvent and a wetting agent. But stripping an entire brick wall is very arduous, and no matter how carefully it is done, paint in the pores of the brick will leave the wall with a variegated appearance.

Preparing for Paint

Removing paint. Hold a paint scraper in one hand and use the heel of the other to exert pressure on the blade as you scrape in the direction of the grain (right). If the paint is difficult to scrape off, you can speed the job with an electric heating iron. Hold the heater in one hand just above the surface. When the softened paint begins to bubble, slip a putty knife under it and scrape it away (far right).

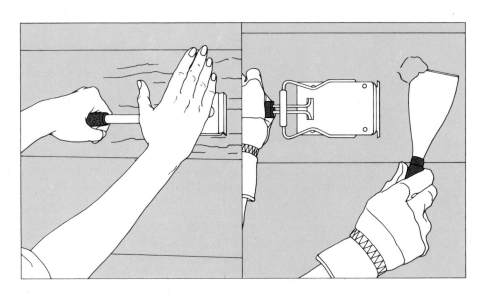

Filling large cracks with oakum. Insert one end of a strip of oakum—use one, two or three strands, depending on the width of the crack—into the widest part of the crack. Working along the length of the crack, jam the oakum tight into the opening with a wood chisel. Pack the crack to within ½ inch of the surface. Fill over the oakum with caulking compound to achieve a smooth surface for painting.

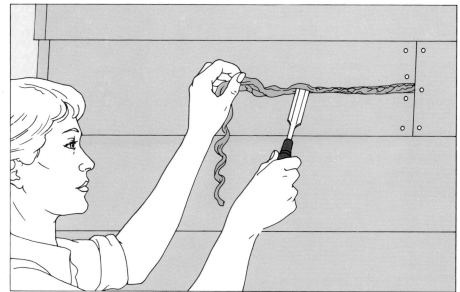

Removing nail rust. Sand a rust-stained area by hand with medium-grade sandpaper or steel wool until all of the rust is removed. Then sand the nailhead itself to remove any built-up rust. Use a nail set to countersink the nailhead. Coat the nailhead and the area around it with paint primer. After the area is dry, fill the countersink hole with exterior wood putty.

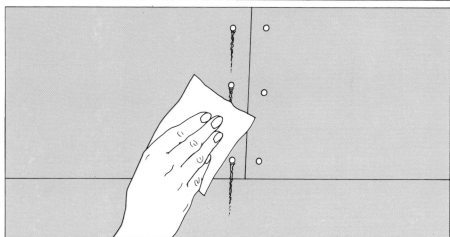

Caulking the joints. Put a cartridge of caulk into a caulking gun and slice off the tip of the cartridge to make an opening about ¼ inch in diameter. Starting in an unobtrusive spot (under a window sill or above a door), pull the trigger of the gun slightly, experimenting with varying pressures to obtain the desired width of the bead. Pull the tip slowly along the joint while squeezing out just enough caulk to fill the joint but not overflow it. (If the caulk does not flow smoothly, warm the cartridge slightly over a hot-air duct or a radiator.)

Use a wet cloth to keep the outside of the cartridge nozzle clear of caulk. Release the trigger just before reaching the end of the seam. Bed the caulking compound into the joint and give a slightly concave shape to its surface, using a wet finger or a damp cloth. Clean away any excess caulking material with a second wet cloth.

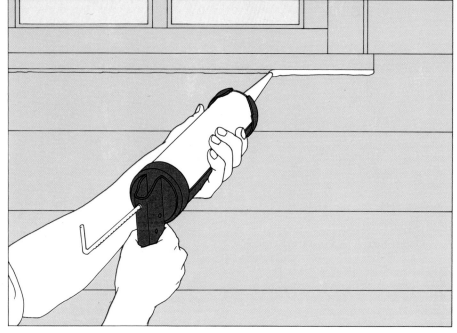

Surface Cleaning for Masonry

Using a pressure washer. Connect a pressure washer to your house cold-water supply with a garden hose. Set the pressure at the lowest level and wet down the wall to soften the dirt. Add a heavy-duty detergent to the tank, in the amount recommended for the machine you have rented, set the pressure between 500 and 1,000 pounds per square inch and, starting at the top, flood the wall surface. Wear goggles and cover any nearby shrubbery when spraying detergents or chemical cleaners. Let the solution soak in for a half hour, then rinse the wall thoroughly with clear water from a garden hose.

Scrubbing brick. To avoid washing old mortar out of the joints between bricks, use a soft-fiber brush and scrub with a circular motion. Try never to scrub back and forth along a mortar line.

Use a handful of mild detergent in a bucket of cold water and scrub only those areas so soiled with soot or other pollutants that they cannot be cleaned satisfactorily with a milder treatment. Rinse the wall well with clean water.

Scraping and brushing. If a brick house has been painted, only drastic methods like sandblasting will strip it, but it is possible to remove spots of paint that dripped onto brick when wood trim above was painted. The tool to use has a wire brush on one side and a scraper on the other. Flip the tool every few strokes, first brushing and then scraping; avoid the mortar joints. Even used with care, the brush may leave the mortar joints with depressions that will need filling.

Using paint remover. After wetting the wall, apply paint remover, taking care to brush in one direction—away from yourself—at all times. Wear goggles, a cap and long sleeves for protection. Let the stripper work 15 to 30 minutes. Then, standing on a ladder, rinse the stripper off thoroughly with a pressure washer or garden hose aimed down and away from yourself.

Sealing damaged brick. Fill a tank-type garden sprayer with a waterproofing solution, available at most paint and hardware stores. Beginning under the eaves, flood the surface evenly. Use the lowest possible pressure, with the nozzle set for a coarse spray, and hold the nozzle close to the wall for maximum control. As you spray, let the sealer run down 5 to 12 inches. Dab off any build-up with a brush. You must cover every square inch of the surface, including all joints; otherwise, some masons say, water will get into the wall and get trapped there by the silicone.

Apply sealer when the air and surface temperature are 50° or higher and the walls have been dry for three full days. Applying a sealer to damp walls will trap salt deposits behind the face of the brick, eventually causing the brick to crumble. Clean the garden sprayer by running turpentine through it; flush the turpentine out with water.

Matching Old Mortar Colors

White portland cement	1 part
Hydrated lime	3 parts
Sand	10 parts

Packing new mortar into the deteriorated joints of an old brick or stone wall—a job called repointing—is done the same way as for a foundation (page 123). But there is one added consideration—color. You will want to match the joints in the rest of the wall.

Old mortars were made with more lime than modern ones and appear much lighter. If yours is more white than gray (and if it feels granular rather than smooth), mix mortar for repointing according to the high-lime recipe at left. The proportions are by volume.

Slowly add just enough water to give the consistency of oatmeal.

Make only a small batch at first, spread it on a piece of scrap wood or an old brick, and let it dry for 12 hours. Then compare it to the color of the mortar in the wall to be repointed. If it is too dark, substitute lighter-colored sand or increase the lime to 4 parts. If it is too light, use darker sand or add a mineral oxide pigment. When working with mortar or any lime, always wear gloves and a long-sleeved shirt to protect your skin.

Patching Holes in Stucco

Properly applied and cured, stucco is a practically indestructible covering for a house. The material dries concrete-hard and has no seams or joints to admit water. Over the years, however, it is likely to develop small cracks or holes. You must patch the damaged areas, or water can enter the wall. While the water will not attack the stucco itself, it can rot the supporting structure within.

You can mix stucco yourself but for small patching jobs it is just as economical to buy it in ready-mixed dry form. Add just enough water to give it a uniform, plastic texture that leaves a fairly heavy residue on your glove but still holds together when picked up and squeezed. Always wear gloves to protect your hands from the lime, and wear goggles to protect your eyes when you pour out the dry mix. If the stucco mix begins to dry out as you work, chop it and mix it with a trowel to restore its proper consistency; do not add water, as it will weaken the mixture.

It is best to patch a stucco wall on a humid, overcast day when the temperature is between 50° and 80°. In any case, the night before you apply the stucco, wet down the area to be patched and then spray it again just before you begin.

1 Filling a hole or crack. After cleaning away any loose debris, apply stucco with a trowel to within ¼ inch of the surface of the wall. If the wall has been exposed down to the lath, use two layers plus a finish coat, letting the first set overnight. Tamp the stucco in firmly as you work.

2 Smoothing the patch. An hour after you apply the second layer, smooth the surface with a small block of wood, using a circular motion. Dampen the patch with a garden hose every 12 hours for the next 48 hours. Then let it dry for two to five days before adding the finish coat.

3 **Applying the final coat.** Dampen the wall and trowel on a finish coat of stucco ⅛ to ¾ inch thick, depending on the texture you must match. Let the stucco set until it just yields to finger pressure, then add the design (*inset*). You can achieve the basic English-cottage stucco pattern by applying thick blobs of stucco over a thin base, then using a twisting motion with a triangular trowel. To create the modern-American pattern, scrape a block of wood in a downward motion over the damp surface of a thin coat of stucco. Achieve a spattered effect by filling a short broom or brush with stucco and hitting it against a stick so that it will spray the stucco onto the wall. To make the travertine pattern, first jab a whisk broom repeatedly into a thick coat of stucco, then smooth out the high points gently with a trowel or wood block.

MODERN-AMERICAN

SPATTERED

TRAVERTINE

Restoring the Integrity of Outside Walls

Exterior walls seem vulnerable to the elements, but they actually are the least trouble-prone structural part of a house. Since water generally runs off these walls immediately, there is little prolonged dampness to nurture rot or to leach lime from old mortar. Wherever you do find rot—for example, in the overhang at the top of a wall, or in wood siding just below the overhang—you usually can trace it to a roof or gutter leak that has allowed moisture to collect on the undersides of exterior boards. In such a case, find and patch the leak that is causing the damage before you make the wall repairs.

Frame houses with wood siding can last for centuries with only minor repairs. But if you notice large flakes of peeling paint, they usually indicate moisture and possibly rot underneath. It is easy enough to replace small rotted sections of siding, if few are involved. Overhang repairs are also simple, though you may need scaffolding to stand on if the overhangs are wide. Even if the interior structural parts are sound, patch holes in the fascia (which covers rafter ends) and in the soffit (which is on the underside of the overhang), if only to keep out birds and squirrels. Paint the backs of replacement boards to prevent future rot.

Window sills, because they are nearly horizontal, sometimes collect water and develop rot. You can correct minor surface defects by scraping away damaged wood, soaking the sill with a wood preservative and applying a fiberglass patch (page 96). For more extensive damage, you can cover the whole sill with aluminum sheathing, painting it to match the house. If rot has badly damaged the sill, you may need to restore the original shape with wood putty before installing either type of patch.

In a masonry wall, the most common failure is the deterioration of the mortar between the bricks or blocks. Even mortar that is well protected from rain can crumble in time because of expansion and contraction caused by temperature changes. To repair such a wall, chip the decaying mortar out of the joints and refill them with new mortar—a job called repointing (page 123).

If bricks over a wall opening have crumbling mortar joints, the bricks may sag or even fall out of the wall. If the bricks were originally laid in a straight course over the opening, you can add steel lintels, a pair of L-shaped bars cut by a metal fabricator to support replacement bricks. Rebuilding a sagging brick arch without a lintel is only slightly more time-consuming. Bricks often collapse over openings where there is no doorframe or window frame to help hold bricks up, as in a garden wall or an open walkway between two row houses. If there is a frame for a door or window in the opening, you need not remove it, but you may have to remove trim molding and knock out some plaster on the inside wall before you can replace the interior courses of bricks over the lintel or arch.

If you must use new bricks to replace broken or missing ones, try to match the old in size and color—some suppliers offer used bricks as well as new ones. Always wear goggles to protect your eyes when you cut a brick, and a hard hat while removing or installing them. When you finish a masonry repair, don rubber gloves and goggles and use muriatic acid to scrub mortar stains from the bricks.

Metal Sheathing for a Worn Wooden Sill

1 Making a template. Use scissors and heavy paper to make templates that will serve as patterns for the ends of an aluminum cover to fit over a damaged window sill. This aluminum sheathing will cover the entire sill and fit between the jambs and around the ears of the sills. The template for each end (inset) must reach from the window stool inside to the underside of the sill and must wrap around the ear of the sill.

Using the templates as patterns, cut .019-inch aluminum sheathing with tin snips; check the fit.

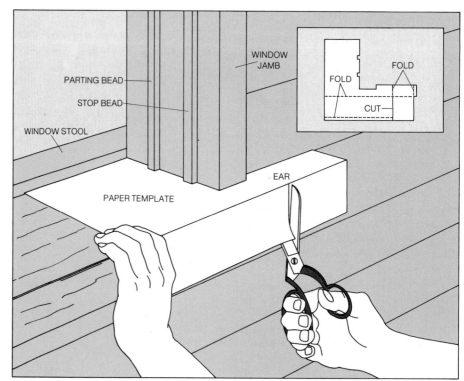

WINDOW JAMB

PARTING BEAD

STOP BEAD

WINDOW STOOL

PAPER TEMPLATE

EAR

FOLD

FOLD

CUT

2 **Caulking the edges.** Use a caulking gun to lay a bead of butyl caulk on and around the sill wherever the cut edges of the metal sheathing will lie—along the window stool, the jambs, the siding, and the underside of the sill.

3 **Securing the sheathing's interior edge.** Position the metal sheathing on the sill, press it into the bead of caulk along the stool, the jambs and the siding, and secure it with roofing nails at 4-inch intervals along the joint of the window sill and stool. Nail the metal in place along the jamb edges and the top of each ear.

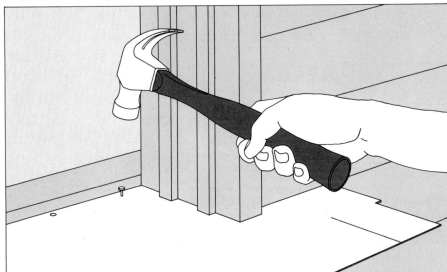

4 **Fitting the sheathing.** Use a rubber mallet to shape the metal around the sill. Start by bending the sheathing and its flaps down over the ends of the ears, then around the sill face, and nail these flaps to the sill face. Finish the shaping by bending the long part of the sheathing over the face of the sill, then up under the bottom; nail it to the bottom. Seal small gaps with caulk, clean the aluminum with metal preparative (available at paint stores), and paint the sheathing with a paint recommended for use on aluminum.

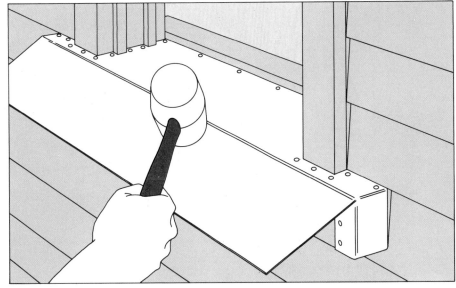

Repairing Rotted Cornices

1 **Cutting away damaged wood.** Starting just beyond an area of damaged wood in a fascia or soffit—the front and bottom parts of the overhanging cornice edging a roof—drill a pilot hole, then use a saber saw or keyhole saw to cut through the board. Avoid sawing into the rafter ends or the so-called lookouts—boards that anchor rafter ends to the house (*below*)—you can find both by looking for the nailheads in the fascia and soffit. Make a second saw cut on the other side of the damaged area. Use a chisel as necessary to complete the two cuts, then pry out the damaged section of board.

2 **Doubling damaged rafter ends.** If a rafter end has rotted, cut a piece of 2-inch-thick lumber to match the shape of the end of the rafter, long enough to reach back to sound wood. Soak it well with wood preservative or use pressure-treated lumber. Nail the new piece alongside the rotted end. If horizontal lookout boards are in the way, remove them before nailing on the new rafter ends. Replace rotted lookouts with new lumber cut to the same dimensions.

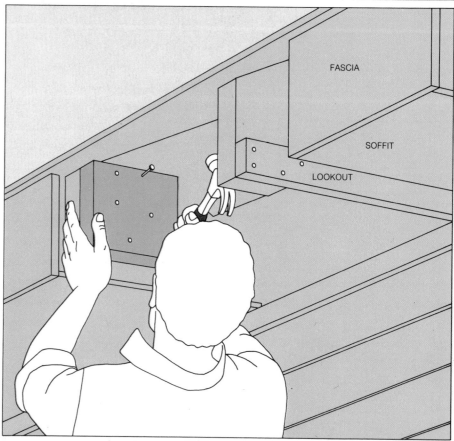

3 **Attaching new fascia or soffit boards.** Using galvanized screws, attach a 1-by-4 wood strip that will overlap the back of the new joint at each edge of the sound part of the fascia or soffit. Screw a replacement section to the strips and nail it to any rafter ends or lookouts that it crosses. Seal the joint at each end with exterior-grade wood putty before you paint.

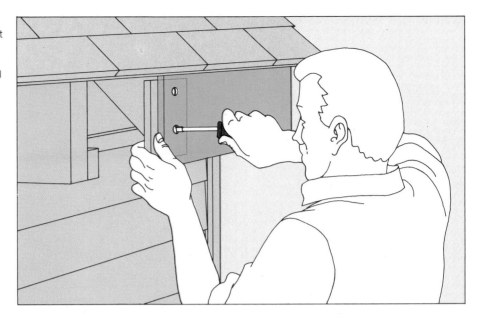

Replacing Damaged Sections of Siding

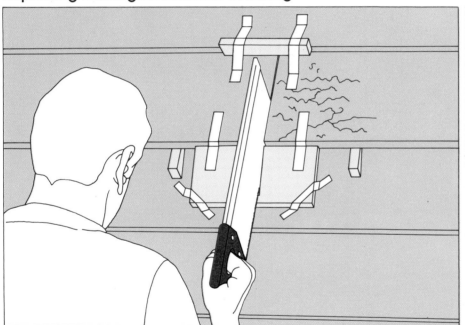

1 **Cutting out damaged clapboard siding.** Tap wedges under a damaged section of clapboard siding to separate it from the piece below, then use a backsaw to cut through it. Protect the boards above and below with wood blocks temporarily held in place with adhesive tape.

2 **Finishing the cut.** Move the wedges to the top of the damaged piece to raise the clapboard above, then finish the cuts, using a keyhole saw with the handle reversed. Use a hacksaw blade to cut through any nails under the damaged piece and remove the piece. Replace it with a new clapboard, driving nails through the lower part just above the top of the clapboard below.

If your siding is made of flush boards, cut out damaged wood with a hammer and chisel and replace it with new wood, using the techniques on pages 54-55 for repairing floorboards. If there is no sheathing beneath the siding, fasten new siding to old with the technique shown above for attaching a new fascia or soffit board.

Supports for Masonry over a Door or Window

1 **Making the shoulders.** Using a cold chisel or brickset and a small sledge, remove two courses of brick above the door or window opening, and enough brick and mortar in these courses on either side to make a ledge, called a shoulder, at least half a brick long on each side. Use a stiff wire brush to clean mortar dust from the shoulder bricks. Dampen them with water and cover them with a ⅜-inch bed of mortar.

2 **Setting the lintel.** After painting two lintels with metal primer, hold them back to back and press them into the mortar on the shoulders. Align the joint between the vertical legs of the lintels with the mortar joint between the face course and the backing course of bricks.

If there is a cavity between the two courses, separate the lintels. Align each vertical leg slightly to the cavity side of the course of bricks below it.

3 Replacing the bricks. Lay a ⅜-inch bed of mortar on the horizontal leg of the outside lintel and apply mortar to the end of a brick. Lay the brick onto the shoulder—partly on the mortar atop the lintel, partly on the mortar atop the lower brick—and tamp it into place until its top is even with the top of the adjacent bricks. Continue laying bricks in the course, and then slide in mortared bricks for the course above. Repeat from the inside of the opening on top of the other lintel.

When there is no cavity between the facing and backing courses, the thickness of the two vertical lintel legs may be greater than the thickness of the mortar joint. To keep bricks atop the lintel from projecting forward, slice off enough of each brick from its back edge *(below)* so it will be flush with the surrounding bricks.

Pack more mortar into the joints with the edge of your trowel. Then use a jointer *(page 123)* to finish all of the mortar joints.

Cutting Bricks to Fit Odd Spaces

To make a square or diagonal piece from the end of a brick *(near right),* use a cold chisel or brickset to cut a groove where you want the brick to separate; turn the brick over and cut a corresponding groove on the opposite face. Place the brick on a bed of sand and strike a sharp blow with the chisel in one of the grooves—the brick will break along the grooves.

To cut an inch off a brick's long side *(far right),* set the brick on end and strike the top end with the blade of a bricklayer's hammer 1 inch from the corner; then turn the brick over and strike the other end in the same way, fracturing the brick lengthwise. Use the blade to clean off rough spots on the cut edges, removing small bits at a time. It is best to practice these techniques on broken bricks before cutting new ones.

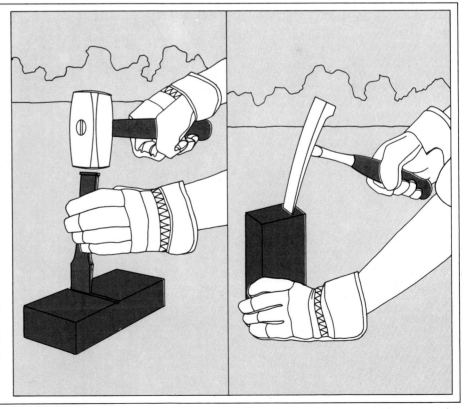

Rebuilding a Brick Arch

1 Making the template. Fasten a piece of ½-inch plywood over the damaged arch. Mark on its face a cross showing where one side of the opening intersects with the lower mortar joint of the course from which the new arch will rise. Make a similar cross for the other side of the opening. Drive nails into each intersection and at points ¼ inch higher. Between the pairs of nails, set the ends of a piece of $^3/_{16}$-inch flexible hardboard or plywood 1 foot longer than the opening width (*inset*). Raise the hardboard at the center to the desired height of the arch, and trace the resulting arc on the plywood, following the bottom edge of the hardboard.

From two pieces of ½-inch plywood, cut two identical templates the shape of the arc, using a saber saw. Trim the bottom straight edges of the templates to connect the ends of the arc. Nail the templates to the opposite ends of 2-inch-thick spacer blocks cut so the completed assembly is slightly less thick than the wall.

HARDBOARD

2 Positioning the bricks. With the template assembly face down on a smooth surface, evenly space an odd number of bricks on end around the curve with a minimum gap of ¼ inch at their lower edges. Position the middle, or key, brick at the exact center of the arch. Mark the brick positions on the template. Find the corner-brick angle by using an adjustable T bevel to duplicate the angle that is formed between the line of the template's straight bottom edge and the outside edge of the end brick in the arch (*inset*).

Set the template into the opening and hold it in position with 2-by-4s fastened with cut nails to bricks at the sides of the opening. If there is a doorframe or window frame already in place, set the template atop the frame.

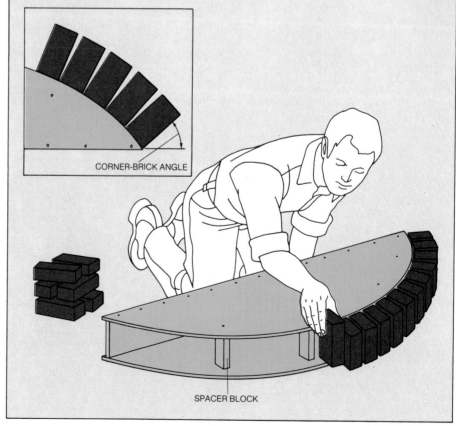

CORNER-BRICK ANGLE

SPACER BLOCK

3 **Laying corner bricks.** Transferring the angle you
set in Step 2, cut a brick to that angle, leaving the
ends of the brick wide enough to complete the
horizontal course at the template's right corner.
Lay mortar for this corner brick, set the brick
in the mortar and tamp it. Cut and set a similar
corner brick for the left side of the arch.

4 **Building the arch.** Lay a bed of mortar on one
corner brick, set the first brick of the arch on
the template, and tamp it firmly into the mortar
until it is aligned with its mark on the template.
Spread mortar thicker at the top than at the bottom, set the next brick and tap it into place.
Continue until you have laid the brick that will be
next to the key brick, then repeat the procedure from the other side of the arch. Lay mortar
on both sides of the key-brick opening, and slide
and tap the key brick up into position.

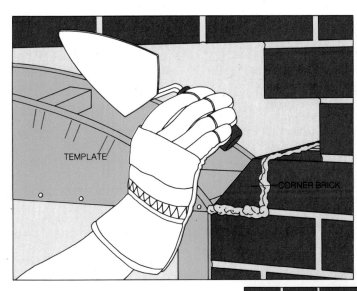

TEMPLATE

CORNER BRICK

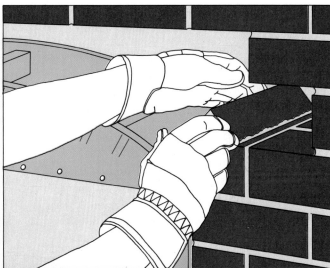

5 **Replacing missing bricks over the arch.** One
at a time, cut filler bricks diagonally to fit in the
horizontal courses above the corner brick. Lay
mortar atop the corner brick and the first bricks in
the arch, apply mortar to the tops and ends of
each filler brick, then slide and tap it into place.
Pack loose joints and finish all joints with a
jointer. Allow the mortar to set for at least 24
hours before removing the template.

Floor Sags: Their Causes and Their Cures

Some structural faults in a floor—especially near staircases, bathtubs and bearing walls—are obvious when an old house is first inspected. Others show up only after a heavy object such as a newly installed refrigerator or a piano has burdened the floor for a few weeks. Sags in the middle of a floor are typically caused by inadequate support from joists and girders below the floor. Sags near an exterior wall, however, indicate rot or insect damage in major structural parts and require more extensive remedies, as shown on the following pages.

Small sags and floors that feel bouncy near the middle of a house will be firmed up temporarily if you shore the floor joists with a framework of beams and supports. To eliminate such sags permanently, however, you must slowly jack the floor back to level, using a telescoping house jack under a floor more than 22 inches above the ground, or a bell-shaped screw jack (page 116) for a low crawl space that is less than 22 inches high. Both types of jack are available at lumberyards and from tool-rental dealers.

Once the floor is level, you may want to leave the jack in place. But if several jacks are required, a more economical solution is to replace each of the jacks with a 4-by-4 post.

Either posts or jacks will obstruct movement around a basement, so you may prefer to reinforce the joists instead. You can stiffen weak joists by nailing new boards to one or both sides. At stairways, strengthen the joints between joists with extra framing members. Beneath bathtubs and heavy radiators, nail solid blocking.

Sags in a wooden girder that spans a basement just beneath the joists call for different solutions. A sag between posts that support the girder can be jacked straight, but to avoid having to insert another post, you must support the joists with temporary shoring on both sides of the girder while you replace the girder with a steel I beam.

A sag at an end of a girder usually indicates rotting or crumbling of a girder pocket—one of the two holes in the foundation wall where the girder ends rest. You can rebuild crumbling girder pockets with ordinary mortar, and shim up some damaged sections of girder, but again, to repair extensive damage you must replace the girder. A sag directly over a post signals rot or an inadequate footing at the base of the post. In this case, instead of inserting extra posts, replace the present post with a steel jack resting on a new concrete footing.

The most vulnerable structural element at the outside edges of the floor in a wood-frame house is the sill plate, often attacked by rot or insects. The weight of the house rests directly on this sill. As the sill crumbles, the floor sags near the exterior walls. Damage extends into the ends of the joists and, in a balloon-frame house, which has long two-story wall studs bearing directly upon the sill, the bottom stud ends are also vulnerable. If you are going to repair or replace any of these parts, you must first jack the joists or studs ¼ inch off the foundation, one side at a time.

A sill that runs at a right angle to the joists, holding up their ends, can be freed with conventional jacking. But one that runs parallel to them requires a different technique: a heavy ledger plank must be nailed to the outside of the wall, parallel with the ground, to be used for jacking up all of the studs.

The replacement sill should closely match the dimensions of the old one, because the mortar bed beneath it can compensate for only about ½ inch of difference. Lumber 2 inches thick, pressure-treated to resist rot, can usually be used. For a very old house, which may have sills as much as 8 inches thick, custom-order timbers from a sawmill and have them pressure-treated.

After the sill has been replaced, end-damaged joists and studs can be reinforced or even replaced; the joists that circle the perimeter of the house are not as difficult to remove as common joists and ordinarily are replaced.

Although a solid-masonry house does not have wooden studs in the exterior walls, its floor joists are still vulnerable to rot and insects—particularly if the ends of the joists are embedded in mortar rather than separated from the masonry by air space. These joists can be jacked up and reinforced in the standard way, but you will need to widen the pockets to allow reinforcing boards to rest on the masonry. Before you attempt to repair the floor of a masonry-veneer house, which has a single layer of masonry over conventional wood studs and thus cannot be jacked without cracking the veneer, consult a structural engineer.

Although to perform any of these repairs you need to lift the house only a fraction of an inch, one side at a time, jacking inevitably risks minor damage to the weakest materials in the walls and floors. Pipes and ducts occasionally rupture and plaster walls sometimes crack or buckle, especially when they contain old cracks that have been filled (open, unfilled cracks in plaster generally close as the floor is lifted and drywall seldom suffers from jacking).

To minimize these hazards, start by disconnecting the joints of any soil stack within 2 feet of the beam you are going to jack up. Jack as large an area at one time as possible so that the floor rises evenly. When straightening the middle of a sagging floor, extend the jack no more than 1/16 inch per day, and never lift the floor more than ½ inch without first obtaining professional advice.

Shoring a Weak Spot

Shoring weak joists. To shore up a floor or a wall above it that runs at a right angle to the joists, lay 10-foot beams of pressure-treated 4-by-4 lumber end to end on the floor of the basement or crawl space. Cut additional pressure-treated 4-by-4 posts 5 inches shorter than the measurement between the floor and the joists. Toenail three posts to each beam, one in the center and one 2 feet in from each end. On a dirt floor, lay a 10-foot pressure-treated 2-by-12 to serve as a "pad" under each beam (on a concrete floor 12-inch pieces of 2-by-8 will do).

With a helper, lift each 4-by-4 framework, horizontal beam on top, and set it on top of its pad. Tap pairs of wood shingle shims between the beam and each joist. Check two adjacent sides of each post with a carpenter's level to see that it is plumb; tap the bottom until the post is perfectly vertical, then toenail it to the pad. Then drive in the shims. Insert an extra post beneath any joint in the beams and toenail the beams together.

To shore a wall parallel to the joists, use a horizontal ledger positioned on the outside of the wall and 2-by-4 posts (*pages 115-116, Steps 1 and 2*).

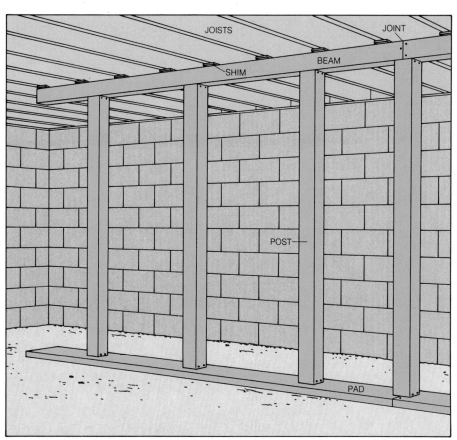

Jacking a sagging girder. With a permanently installed house jack, you can easily straighten a girder that is sagging in the middle. Set a 4-by-8 pad 3 feet long beneath the lowest point of the sag. Put a telescoping house jack on the pad, extend its upper tube to the girder and lock the tube with the two steel pins provided. Turn the jacking screw at the bottom until the top of the jack presses snugly against the girder. Plumb two adjacent sides of the jack with a carpenter's level, tap the jack sideways until it is perfectly vertical, and nail the flat steel plates at each end to the girder and to the pad. (If the girder is sagging over a supporting post, set pads on each side of the post and use two jacks until you can replace the defective post.)

Tighten the jack 1/16 inch each day—roughly 1/8 turn on most models. If the jacking screw is stiff, oil the threads and slide a pipe over the handle for more leverage. Check the ends of the girder—if they begin to rise, the jack is lifting the entire girder rather than straightening the sag. Stop jacking for a few days and moisten the girder with a garden sprayer to increase its flexibility. When the sag disappears, remove the jack handle and glue the threads with epoxy to prevent anyone from carelessly removing the jack.

Jacking an Outside Wall that Crosses the Joists

1 Preparing the wall. The first step in removing a damaged sill plate for replacement is to unscrew nuts and remove washers from any anchor bolts that fasten the wooden sill to the foundation; if the sill and joists are fastened with metal straps, remove them as well. On the outside of the house, use a pry bar to remove horizontal lengths of siding and sheathing wide enough to expose the sill plate, the joists and the lower ends of the wall studs.

If your house has balloon framing (*page 9*), with studs that rest beside the joists on the sill plate, make sure the joists and studs are fastened together with at least four 16-penny nails (*inset*); add extra nails if necessary.

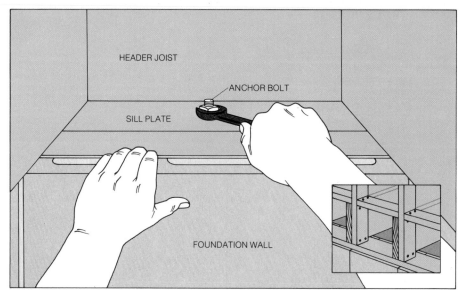

HEADER JOIST

ANCHOR BOLT

SILL PLATE

FOUNDATION WALL

2 Setting up the jack. Starting at one side of the basement, toenail a 4-by-4 beam about 10 feet long in place underneath the joists; run the beam parallel with the foundation wall and about 18 inches from it. Lay a 10-foot 2-by-12 pad on the floor beneath the 4-by-4. On this pad, center a telescoping house jack and tighten it just enough to hold it in place.

If the width of the joists varies, insert wooden shims between any narrower joist and the beam; the combined width of a joist and its shim should match the width of the widest joist.

3 Jacking the beam. Slowly tighten the jack until the floor above is level. To test, set a carpenter's level on the floor, at a right angle to the wall nearest the jack, and have a helper watch it as you tighten the jack. When the floor is level, measure the space between the joists and the foundation wall at points near the jack; this is how thick a replacement sill should be. Then slowly raise the jack an additional ¼ inch. Proceed with care; sometimes one half turn is enough.

4 **Supporting the beam.** Cut a 4-by-4 post to fit exactly between the pad and the beam, alongside the jack, and slide the post into place. Then tap wood shims between the post and the beam. Make sure the post is plumb, drive the shims in and remove the jack. Sight along the beam from one end to determine whether the ends are bowing down from the weight of the house. If they are, set up the jack 2 feet from one end of the beam, jack that end level with the center of the beam and insert another 4-by-4 post there. Jack and support the other end in the same way.

Using additional 10-foot beams the same way, jack up the remaining joists along the wall and support them with additional posts.

Jacking an Outside Wall that Parallels the Joists

1 **Securing the ledgers.** Prepare the wall for jacking by loosening anchor bolts and removing some siding and sheathing; then, starting at one corner, nail horizontal 2-by-6 planks called ledgers, each 10 feet long, to the wall studs 3 feet above the sill plate. Drive two 20-penny nails through the ledger and siding into each stud. Level the ground near the foundation wall and lay 2-by-12 pads on the ground beneath the ledgers.

2 **Jacking the ledger wall.** Set a bell jack—a screw jack about 1 foot tall with a bell-shaped cast-iron body—on the pad. Cut a 4-by-4 to fit between the jack and the bottom edge of the ledger and have a helper hold the 4-by-4 while you tighten the jack. Jack the ledger until the stud is ¼ inch above where the top of the new sill will be, then cut a 2-by-4 to fit between the ledger and the pad. Place the top of the 2-by-4 flat against the siding and beneath the ledger, and drive the bottom tight onto the pad with a hammer (*inset*). Toenail the 2-by-4 to the pad. Remove the bell jack, then use it to jack under the ledgers so that it supports each remaining stud in the same fashion.

Replacing a Sill Plate

1 **Cutting out part of the old sill.** Pry the rotted sill slightly away from the header or stringer joist above it with a utility bar. Then cut horizontally along the top of the sill with a rented demolition saw fitted with a blade designed to cut through nails embedded in wood. Sever the toenails that fasten the sill to the header or stringer joist, to the common joists and, in a balloon-frame house, to the bottom ends of the studs. At each end of the rotted portion of the sill, cut vertically through the sill midway between two anchor bolts; then make vertical cuts on both sides of each intermediate bolt. Knock out the cut pieces of sill with a hammer.

Inspect the joists that rested on the sill for rot or insect damage. If you have a balloon-frame house, inspect the ends of the studs as well. Reinforce or replace any damaged joists (*pages 118-119*) or stud ends (*pages 120-121*).

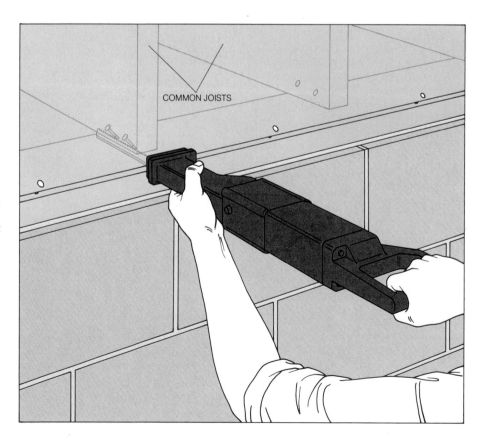

2 **Notching the new sill.** Have a helper hold the
new sill section on the foundation wall from
the outside while you mark the location of each
anchor bolt from inside. For sills more than 12
feet long, use several pieces of lumber cut so the
joints are midway between anchor bolts. At
each anchor-bolt mark, cut a rounded notch to let
the sill slide around the bolt. Use a saber saw
to notch sills that are as much as 1½ inches thick,
a demolition saw for thicker ones.

If the anchor bolts are corroded beyond use,
cut halfway through each with a hacksaw or the
demolition saw, flush with the top of the foundation. Then snap the bolt along the cut by hitting
the top sideways with a hammer.

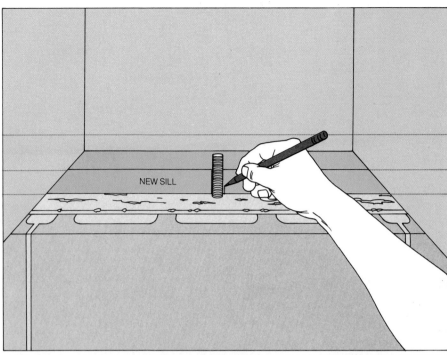

NEW SILL

3 **Preparing the foundation.** If the mortar bed
beneath the old sill is crumbling or the new sill is
thinner than the old one, loosen the old mortar with a cold chisel and clean it off with a wire
brush. Wet the foundation, then spread a new
bed of mortar on the foundation. Use spalls—bits
of brick or concrete block—to hold the new sill
at the correct height and to keep it from squeezing the wet mortar out. Place the spalls in the
mortar every 4 inches, then proceed to Step 4.

If the mortar is sound or absent, skip this step;
no new mortar is required.

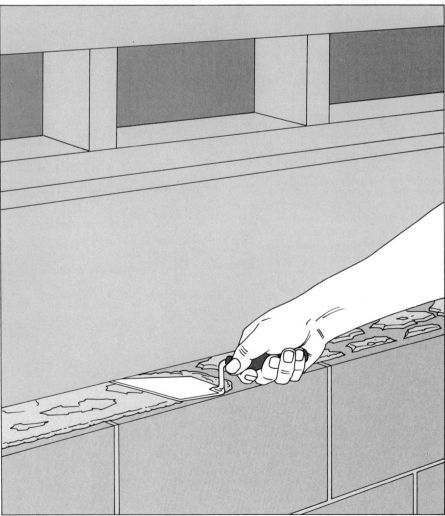

4 Fastening the new sill. Slide the new sill section onto the old anchor bolts. If you are using new mortar, tap the sill down onto it, check the sill with a carpenter's level and let the mortar set for one day. Slide oversized washers over the anchor bolts, then tighten the original nuts securely (*left inset*). By lowering the jacks, release the joists or studs into their original positions; then toenail them to the new sill.

If your house does not have anchor bolts or you had to cut them off, use tie straps to serve their function. After you lower the joists or studs and toenail them to the sill, bolt twisted 12-gauge steel tie straps (*right inset*) to the foundation with ½-inch lag bolts and lead expansion anchors. Place a strap beneath every third joist and nail the straps to the joists.

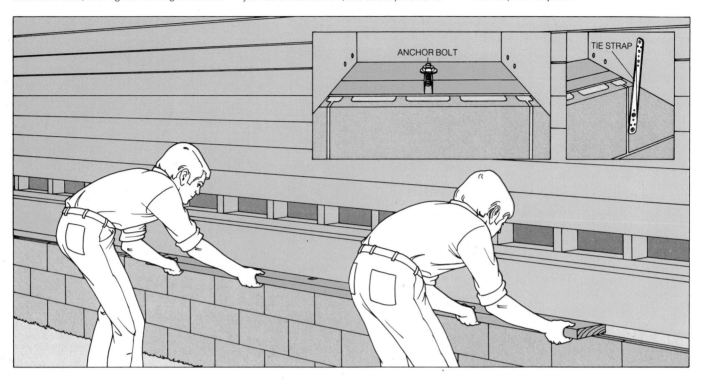

ANCHOR BOLT

TIE STRAP

Repairs for Joists in a Frame House

Reinforcing a rotted joist. Remove any pipes, ducts, electrical cables or wood bracing on one side of the rotted joist, and set a 2-inch-thick board of the same width beside it. Make sure the ends of the new board and old joist are aligned at the wall, and the new board is tight against the subfloor above it. Then fasten the two together with staggered 16-penny nails every 12 inches. If damage extends more than 2 inches, but not into the unsupported middle span of the joist, use a supporting board at least one fourth as long as the joist; a longer board is better. If the damage extends into the joist span but is less than $1/10$ of the span, reinforce at least half the length of the joist. More extensive rot requires a reinforcing board the full length of the old joist.

An end damaged slightly—in an area less than 1 inch high and 2 inches long—can be reinforced (*inset*) without adding a board if the span of the joist is intact. Jack the joist level, chisel away the damaged portion until you reach solid wood, and cut a wooden block to replace the damaged section. Drive it into the gap between the joist and the sill and toenail it in place.

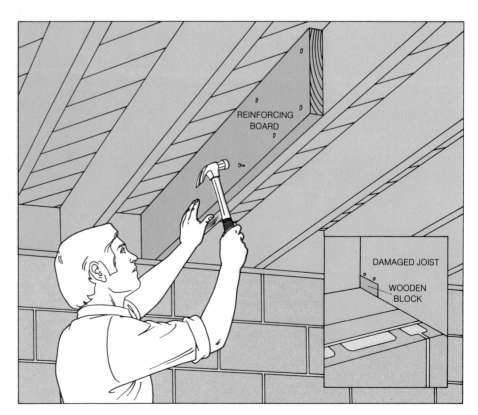

REINFORCING BOARD

DAMAGED JOIST

WOODEN BLOCK

Replacing header or stringer joists. Jack up the joists or wall studs. Then, to replace a damaged header joist crossing the ends of common joists, nail solid blocks of wood between the common joists, 5 feet from the foundation unless there is already wood bracing or blocking near that point. Using a demolition saw, cut horizontally between the subfloor and the header joist to free it from the sole plate and then cut out the rotted section. From underneath the floor, knock out the old header joist with a 2-by-4 and a light sledge hammer. Cut a replacement header joist to the same length and width as the old one and fasten it to the end of each common joist with four 16-penny nails.

To install a new stringer joist, cut the old one out the same way but knock it free from outside. Then slide the new joist into position and toenail the sole plate of the wall above to it.

On a header joist, the joints ordinarily fall on the ends of common joists; if here they do not—or if you decide to replace a small section of header joist—nail a solid block between the common joists behind the joint (*left inset*). To join the pieces of a new stringer joist, nail a block of wood across the joint (*right inset*).

HEADER JOIST   BLOCK

BLOCK   STRINGER JOIST

Repairs for Joists in a Masonry House

Enlarging a masonry joist pocket. To accommodate the added thickness of a reinforced joist in a solid-masonry house, jack the joist until it is level (*pages 114-115*). Using a cold chisel and a sledge hammer, chip out the masonry on both sides of the joist to create a ½-inch space. Extend the pocket another 1½ inches on one side to make space for the reinforcing board.

Making a fire cut. All the old joists that are set in pockets in a solid-masonry wall have ends that are cut at an angle. In the event of a fire, the angled ends of collapsing joists will slip out of their pockets, preventing the joists from pulling down the wall. Hence, the end of a reinforcing board for a rotted joist must also be cut at an angle. Draw a diagonal line at one end of such a board from the lower corner to a point 3 inches in from the upper corner. Cut the board along this line, then nail it to the old joist.

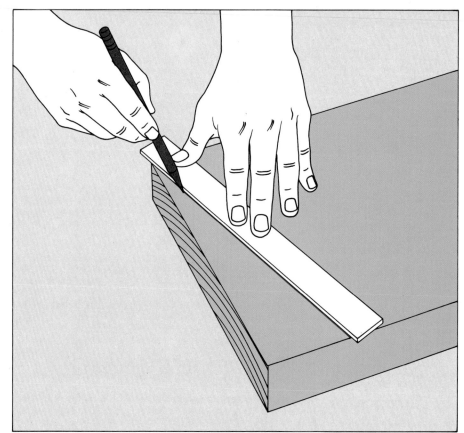

Splints for Rotted Studs

1 Cutting off the rotted ends. Jack up both the wall studs and the joists and replace the sill plate (*pages 114-118*), then remove at least 2 feet of the lower siding and sheathing from the house and knock out the fire stops nailed between the studs. Using a demolition saw, cut off the rotted end of each stud, above the visibly rotted portion. Split away the cut end with a hammer and a wood chisel and drive out protruding nails. Paint the remaining stud end with wood preservative, soaking the wood thoroughly.

2 Propping up the studs. For each stud, cut a wooden filler block as wide and as thick as the stud to fit into the space left by the section you have removed, but with its lower end ¼ inch above the sill plate to allow for the ¼ inch that the studs have been jacked up. Fasten it in place with two eightpenny nails.

3 Reinforcing the studs. Slide a new piece of wood that matches the thickness of the stud and is at least 1 foot long—a longer board is better if it will fit—into the wall alongside the stud. Set the lower end of the new board even with the bottom of the filler block and fasten it to the stud and the filler block with staggered 16-penny nails every 6 inches.

When all of the rotten stud ends have been replaced and all the filler blocks have been reinforced, lower the jacks and, one at a time, reposition the studs and the joists on the new sill plate. Toenail them to the sill plate and nail new fire stops between the studs.

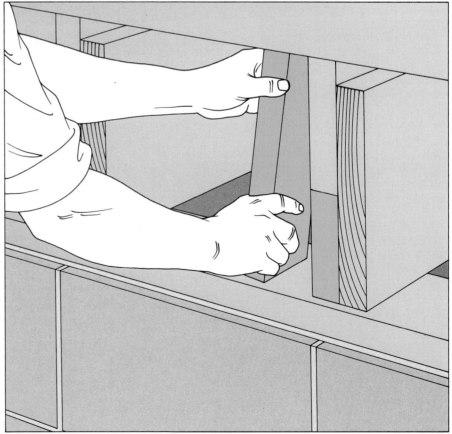

Fixing Foundations that Have Cracked or Settled

Foundations, whether built of stone, brick, concrete block or poured concrete, quite often develop a multitude of minor flaws as they age: small cracks, the result of years of settling and shrinking; crumbling joints, caused by the use of mortar that was made with too much sand or with lime rather than portland cement; even a few broken pieces of masonry. All these problems are structurally harmless, but you may want to repair them anyway—particularly if they are visible outside the house or if they let water into the basement or crawl space.

Before attempting to seal the walls against water—a difficult and somewhat problematical job—check the gutters, downspouts and grading around the house, to make sure they are not funneling water toward the foundation. Repairs in these places often entirely eliminate dampness inside. In the basement, try covering the foundation wall with a waterproof paint to prevent water from seeping through porous masonry.

The next recourse is to fix visible cracks and faults in the masonry. To determine whether a crack is stationary or flexes seasonally as the ground outside expands when frozen and contracts when thawed, mark the ends and center of the crack and measure its width at the center marks, then check the measurements each month from winter to summer.

A dry, stationary crack can be filled with patching mortar or epoxy resin. A constantly leaking crack must be patched with hydraulic cement, a type of mortar that hardens even in the presence of water. A crack that expands and contracts can be filled with mastic joint sealer. All of these patching materials are widely available at building-supply stores. Soften the mastic with a propane torch and

press it into the crack with a putty knife, then cover it with patching mortar. In a concrete-block wall, the crack may reach the hollow core of the block; chisel out the crack and stuff expansion-joint material (the flexible, asphalt-impregnated board used at the joints of a concrete sidewalk) into the crack until the core is filled, then apply the mastic joint sealer.

If all of these measures fail to stem the flow of water, you can resort to a heroic solution: excavate outside down to the footing, waterproof the outside of the wall with a ½-inch layer of bituminous asphalt, and lay gravel and perforated drain tile around the footing. You may well consider this a job for a professional.

In a very old house, small parts of the foundation wall may be crumbling because of bad mortar or deteriorating brick. This condition does not pose an immediate structural threat, but widespread crumbling eventually will allow uneven settling and cause sagging floors, cracked walls and sticking doors.

A brick foundation ordinarily has two or three thicknesses, called wythes; small parts of the inner wythe (or, in extreme cases, the entire inner wythe) can be rebuilt section by section, either with old brick or stone or with new masonry that matches the old dimensions. Even the outer wythe can be rebuilt, but to get at the underground portion you will need to have a backhoe operator excavate around the house. Excavations deeper than 3 feet require not only a backhoe but the advice of an engineer; they may need special shoring to prevent hazardous cave-ins.

A stone or concrete-block wall can be rebuilt in the same way, but these projects also require extensive excavation and the advice of an engineer.

The most serious problem in an old foundation is uneven settling, usually accompanied by large vertical cracks (more than ⅛ inch wide and 4 feet long), particularly near windows and corners. Uneven settling has a variety of causes: an inadequate footing (or none at all) at the base of the wall; a footing built above the frost line, where shifting earth can move it; or weak soil—notably loose fill, or soils high in loam, peat, silt and clay. The solution is to underpin part or all of the old foundation with a new footing, as prescribed by a soil or foundation engineer. If you wish, you can rebuild a crumbling foundation wall at the same time and, in extreme cases, you can jack a tilted floor until it is level and replace a rotted sill plate *(pages 112-118)*.

Underpinning is not a complicated chore and it can be done over a period of weeks or months, but it does involve very heavy work. You will need to dig short trenches beneath the old foundation, then fill them with steel reinforcing rods and concrete while the rest of the foundation supports the house; and finally, pack any gaps between the new footing and old foundation with an almost-dry mixture of sand and cement.

To get beneath the foundation of a crawl-space house, hire a backhoe operator to dig a trench 4 feet wide all around the house, then dig short trenches for the new footings by hand. If the house has a basement, it is usually easier to work from inside, jackhammering through a concrete floor or digging up a dirt floor. If you are filling more than five trenches with concrete at one time, have a transit-mix company deliver the concrete—via a chute through the basement window if necessary. For smaller batches, rent a portable concrete mixer.

Patching and Pointing

Patching a crack. Chisel around a crack in concrete block with a cold chisel and a light sledge hammer, making an inverted V-shaped groove (wider on the inside) about ½ inch deep, ½ inch wide at the face of the wall and 1 inch wide at the back. Clean this groove with a wire brush, wet it and use a pointing trowel to press a thin coat of patching mortar into it. Wait a minute, then spread more mortar over the groove and tamp the mortar tightly into the crack with a ball-peen hammer or scrap board. Smooth the surface of the mortar with the trowel and rub it with a piece of damp burlap to give it a texture matching that of the block.

Cover the mortar with a sheet of flexible plastic and allow it to cure for three days, lifting the plastic and sprinkling the mortar with water from time to time to keep it damp.

Repointing crumbling mortar. To prepare the joints, chisel out the old mortar to a depth of 1 inch and spray the joints lightly with water. Press new mortar into each joint with a joint filler, sliding the mortar over a mason's hawk held just below the joint. Finish the joints to match the rest of the wall, pressing the mortar into the joints with a mason's jointer (or its homemade equivalent): a convex jointer (or a teaspoon) for concave joints; a V-jointer (or the tip of a trowel) for V-shaped joints; a trowel for flush joints.

Replacing a broken brick. Chisel out the mortar around a broken brick, then split the brick into several pieces to remove it. Chisel out any mortar behind the brick, being careful not to damage nearby bricks; wire-brush the pocket left by the old brick. Cut 1 inch off the back of a new brick (page 109) so that the brick will have ample room at the back; wet the pocket and mortar its sides, then mortar each side of the

brick. Hold the brick on a board and push it off the board and into the pocket with your hand; tap the brick into position, using the butt of a trowel handle. Mortar the joints (left).

To replace a broken concrete block, chisel out the front half of the block; leave the back half intact. Mortar a solid 4-by-8-by-16 block into the pocket left by the thicker broken block.

Rebuilding part of a foundation. Rebuild the damaged portion of a brick or block foundation wall in sections no more than 3 feet wide, working from one side of the damaged portion to the other. If the sections that you plan to replace are more than 2 feet down from the joists above, chisel out the bricks or blocks over the width of the section, working from top to bottom. The wall will form an arch over the opening to carry the load as you remove the masonry underneath, leaving a zigzag pattern of old but sound masonry on each side. To remove bricks or blocks nearer the joists, support the joists (or, in a nonbearing wall, support the studs of the wall above) with shoring *(pages 112-113)* before you remove the masonry.

Lay the new courses of bricks or blocks in the opening, adjusting the thickness of mortar joints to match the spacing in adjacent masonry. Allow the mortar to harden and cure for three days, then chisel out and replace the next section of foundation that is damaged.

Underpinning a Foundation Wall

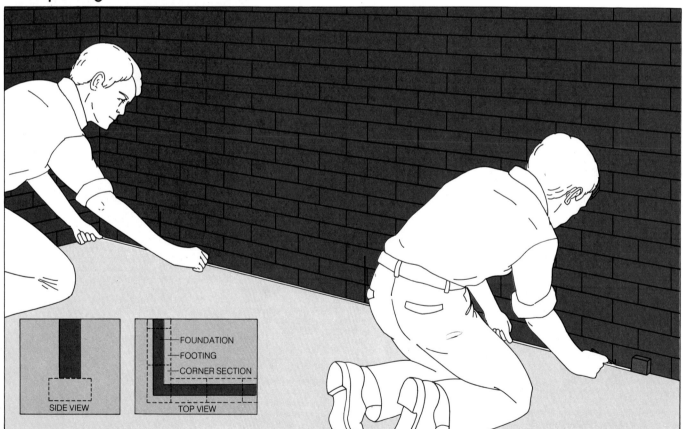

SIDE VIEW

FOUNDATION
FOOTING
CORNER SECTION

TOP VIEW

1 **Laying out the new footing.** Working on the dirt floor of a basement or crawl space—you may have to jackhammer out a part of a concrete basement floor first—mark each foundation wall about 2 feet from each corner, then mark equal sections no more than 4 feet long on the re-maining length of wall *(right inset)*. Starting next to a corner section, dig beneath the old foot-ing or foundation wall in one marked section, to dimensions specified by a foundation engineer or your building code—typically twice as wide as the foundation wall and as deep as the width of the wall *(left inset)*. If necessary, remove extra dirt on the near side of the wall to gain access to the far edge of the footing. Dig out other marked sections along each wall, leaving at least 12 feet of undisturbed earth between excavated sections. Do not dig the corner sections yet.

2 **Installing reinforcing bars.** With a small sledge hammer, drive two 32-inch No. 4 steel reinforcing bars horizontally into the dirt at each end of the excavations. Place the bars about 3 inches from the trench bottom and directly below each side of the wall. Drive each bar about halfway.

If the foundation engineer or your local building code requires a continuous span of reinforcing bars through each trench section, use tie wire to splice long bars lengthwise to protruding pairs of bars in each section. Make the ends of the bars overlap 16 inches at each joint.

Dampen the trench section with a hose, then fill it with a stiff mixture of concrete; drive a shovel into the concrete repeatedly to force it under the wall and to eliminate air bubbles. Leave about 2 inches between the underside of the old foundation and the top of the new concrete.

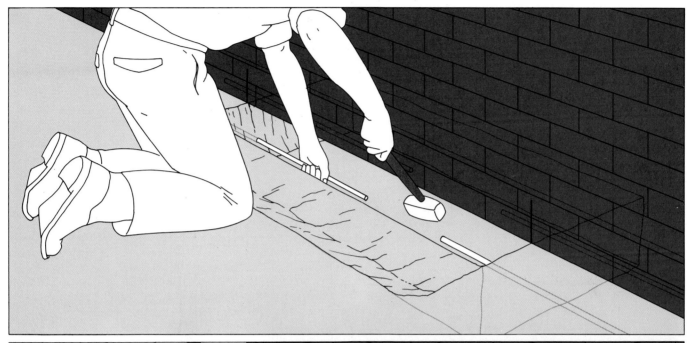

3 **Dry-packing the footing.** Let the concrete set for a day, then make a dry-pack mixture of 1 part portland cement, 3 parts sand, and barely enough water to let the mixture hold its shape when you squeeze it in your hand. Trowel the dry pack into the gap between each footing section and the old wall above, then pack it in tightly by driving the end of a 1- or 2-inch board

into the gap with a sledge hammer. Add and pack mortar until the gaps are completely filled; cover the footing and the dry pack with plastic sheets and let them cure for one week, sprinkling them with water occasionally.

When the dry pack has cured for two days, dig and pour the next set of midwall footing sections

in the same way (*Steps 1-2*), digging no closer than 12 feet from any excavated, unfilled section and dry-packing each one.

After all of the midwall sections have been poured, then dig, pour and dry-pack the corner sections. Replace those sections of the concrete floor that you had to dig up.

Picture Credits

Sources for illustrations are below. The drawings were created by Jack Arthur, Roger C. Essley, William J. Hennessy Jr., Fred Holz, Dick Lee, John Martinez, Joan McGurren and Bill McWilliams. Other credits from left to right are separated by semicolons, top to bottom by dashes. Cover: Fil Hunter. 6: Fil Hunter. 8, 9: Ray Skibinski. 11: Ray Skibinski—Greg Schaler. 12-21: Ray Skibinski. 24: Fil Hunter. 26-33: John Massey. 34-41: Walter Hilmers Jr. 42-49: Frederic F. Bigio from B-C Graphics. 50-55: Ray Skibinski. 56-63: Eduino Pereira. 64: John Massey. 65: Bill McWilliams. 66: Fil Hunter. 68-71: Elsie Hennig. 72-75: Frederic F. Bigio from B-C Graphics. 76-81: John Massey. 82-87: Frederic F. Bigio from B-C Graphics. 88: Fil Hunter. 90, 91: Snowden Associates, Inc. 92-95: Walter Hilmers Jr. 96, 97: Snowden Associates, Inc. 98-103: Peter McGinn. 104-111: Forte, Inc. 112-121: Frederic F. Bigio from B-C Graphics. 122-125: Terry Atkinson.

Acknowledgments

The index/glossary for this book was prepared by Louise Hedberg. The editors also wish to thank the following: Glen C. Baker, Alexandria, Virginia; Philip K. Blumer, Dow Corning Corporation, Midland, Michigan; David Bower, Designs in Wood, Palo Alto, California; Arthur C. Brooks, Stanley Power Tools, New Bern, North Carolina; Kevin Callaghan, National Concrete Masonry Association, Herndon, Virginia; Melvin Chappell, Vienna, Virginia; Basilio Ciocci, Washington, D.C.; Michael Clark, Brooklyn, New York; Roger S. Clarke, Architect, Hartford, Connecticut; Charles Crocker, Arlington, Virginia; Keith Decker, Jack's Roofing Co., Inc., Bethesda, Maryland; Marlaina Deppe, Handwork Gallery, New York City; Thomas A. Downey Jr., P.E., Thomas Downey, Ltd., Alexandria, Virginia; Felber Studios, Ardmore, Pennsylvania; Otto Fenn, Sag Harbor, New York; Mrs. Bernard Fensterwald, Alexandria, Virginia; Florence and Lou Fink, Sag Harbor, New York; Robert L. Giannetti, Brentwood, Maryland; David Girt and James Widner, Metropolitan Chimney, Silver Spring, Maryland; Martin Harp, Alexandria, Virginia; Frederick and May Hill, New York, New York; Hytla & Hart, Washington, D.C.; Mickey Irwin, Jack T. Irwin, Inc., Rockville, Maryland; Henry M. Jones, Alexandria, Virginia; S. K. Kelso Sons Inc., Ardmore, Pennsylvania; Michael Kempster and Robert Sweeney, Dovetail Company, Sudbury, Massachusetts; Lawrence Kennedy, Thomas Edison High School, Alexandria, Virginia; Roberta and Kenneth Kistler, Stamfordville, New York; Harry Kroll, District Lock & Hardware Co., Washington, D.C.; James Kuryloski, Havertown, Pennsylvania; Dan Loewenthal, Bethesda, Maryland; R. Kent Mather, John Carl Warnecke & Associates, San Francisco; Ron Mazzeo, Mazzeo's Chimney Service, Rockland, Maine; Raymond Mitchell, Rockville, Maryland; Mike Moore, The Strip Joint, Alexandria, Virginia; M. Hamilton Morton Jr., A.I.A., Washington, D.C.; Stephen Olson, Tjerlund Products, Inc., St. Paul, Minnesota; Stonewall O'Meara, Alexandria, Virginia; Jim Papile, Alexandria, Virginia; Armistead Perry, Eugene W. Zimmerman and Martyn Zimmerman, Eugene W. Zimmerman Corp., Alexandria, Virginia; Michael Pigott, Hamilton Welding & Iron, Inc., Springfield, Virginia; Richard Lee Plumley, Washington, D.C.; Tim Prentice, Architect, New York City; Theodore H. M. Prudon, Senior Research Associate and Lecturer, Columbia University School of Architecture, New York City; Frank Ramey, Fannon Petroleum Services, Inc., Alexandria, Virginia; Valerie and Steve Resnick, Glasscrafters, Alexandria, Virginia; Arlene Robach, Barbara Held Inc., Washington, D.C.; Elsa Rosenthal, Artifacts, Inc., Alexandria, Virginia; John Rust, Alexandria, Virginia; Schnabel Foundation Co., Bethesda, Maryland; Mr. and Mrs. William Seale, Alexandria, Virginia; Stanley H. Smith, Stevens Institute of Technology, Hoboken, New Jersey; Andy Solinar, D & S Repair Service, Alexandria, Virginia; Frances and Paul Spaulding, The Carriage Trade, Ltd., Alexandria, Virginia; Philip Spiess, National Trust for Historic Preservation, Washington, D.C.; Richard E. Swibold, A.I.A., Collinsville, Connecticut; R. J. Turner, Turner Real Estate, Washington, D.C.; Urbas and Izzo, Rockville, Maryland; Captain and Mrs. E. K. Van Swearingen, Alexandria, Virginia; Robert M. Vogel, Curator, Division of Mechanical and Civil Engineering, Smithsonian Institution, Washington, D.C.; Winston Whitney, Bethesda, Maryland; Gordon Whittington, Vicksburg, Mississippi; Dave Williams, Architect, Amherst, Massachusetts. The editors are indebted to Patricia Bangs, Victoria W. Monks and Wendy Murphy, writers, for their help.

Index/Glossary

Included in this index are definitions of many of the technical terms used in this book. Page references in italics indicate an illustration of the subject mentioned.